THE
DOUBLEDAY
CODE

How to Become a Catholic Major Leaguer

JIM PIECZYNSKI

Illustrations by Chris Pelicano

Copyright © 2021 by Jim Pieczynski. Published 2021 by Our Sunday Visitor, Inc.

26 25 24 23 22 21   1 2 3 4 5 6 7 8 9

ISBN: 978-1-68192-672-8 (Inventory No. T2539)
1. RELIGION—Christian Living—Personal Growth.
2. RELIGION—Christian Living—Men's Interests.
3. RELIGION—Christianity—Catholic.

LCCN: 2021943361

Cover & interior design: Gina Rivera Fickett
Interior art: Chris Pelicano

Printed in the United States of America

... batting clean-up from Houston,
Tom Thibodeau, a spiritual motivator
and RBI leader for the Kingdom ...

You've got to be very careful if you don't know where you are going because you might not get there.

— Yogi Berra

Remember that you have only one soul; that you have only one death to die; that you have only one life, which is short and has to be lived by you alone; and there is only one Glory, which is eternal. If you do this, there will be many things about which you care nothing.

— St. Teresa of Ávila

CONTENTS

PREFACE

I grew up in the small, northeast Pennsylvania town of West Wyoming. Two events converged in May 1963 that provided the seeds for this book.

As an eight-year-old, big for my age, I played in my first Little League game. I was sent to the mound to pitch against players as old as twelve. After a wild first inning, I continued to struggle, walking the first batter in the second. Then I hit Joe Ostrowski Jr. in the back with my best fastball. (Joe Ostrowski! The Little Leaguer's father, Joe Ostrowski Sr. was West Wyoming's pride, having pitched for the New York Yankees.)

After yet another walk, our manager dispatched me to left field.

The next batter hit a single down the left field line. I charged, fielded the ball, and fired to home. Wouldn't you know it? As he rounded third, I hit Joe Ostrowski Jr. square in the back again!

Still, this unpromising beginning, after a few more successful outings, led to my lifetime love of the game, while my first Little League story became part of family lore.

That same month, I also received my first holy Communion. In that moment I felt a "special" call from Our Lord. Years later, this calling spurred me to teach high school CCD for over a decade, then serve as an RCIA instructor, and finally offer talks to Catholic men's groups. It was for one such talk in 1999 that I combined my two loves into a presentation entitled, "Baseball and Baptism."

I have a threefold purpose in offering these reflections on how baseball, by analogy, suggests fundamental truths of the Catholic faith. The first is that over the years the presentation grew and grew, culminating in requests for the written version you now hold in your hands.

The second and most important reason lies in my hope that the reader's passionate love of baseball may enkindle an even more passionate love for Jesus Christ and the Holy Catholic Church; an overwhelming desire to become a Catholic Major Leaguer.

My third purpose — or hope — is that those who come to see the deeper realities of God's through this will be kind enough to say a prayer for the author.

So, let's explore the simplicity and complexity of this wonderful game from an otherworldly perspective. The goal is to appreciate not only the passing joys of earthly baseball seasons but even more to embrace the eternal truth and beauty of the Catholic Faith. Let the natural lead to the supernatural. Let all our desires and enthusiasm lead to a career ending in the eternal Hall of Fame — HEAVEN.

INTRODUCTION

In the beginning, God created the heavens and the earth.

— Genesis 1:1

The first verse of Sacred Scripture leads to the story of the creation of the world, the human race, and the Hebrew people. If you think about it, since all of human history followed from this event, it is here that God also laid the foundation for opening day of baseball season.

When did baseball's genesis, its "big inning," take place? When was the first contest between competing nines that we so affectionately call the national pastime?

Did Abner Doubleday, as is sometimes commonly thought, really give us this magnificent sport?

Like the story of creation, Doubleday's connection to baseball is shrouded in mystery. Most baseball fans easily recognize the name associated with the game's origins, but there is precious little evidence to substantiate the claim. Somehow (perhaps through a story concocted by A. G. Spalding of sporting goods company fame) Doubleday was credited with organizing the first game played on Phinney's farm in Cooperstown, New York, in 1839.

The problem is Doubleday was a student at West Point that year.

Doubleday graduated from West Point and become a career US Army officer. In fact, Doubleday was stationed at Fort Sumter and, in 1861, directed the Union's first shot against the Confederacy.

He did not, however, Direct the first baseball pitch in 1839. Moreover, Doubleday's writings and correspondence never referred to his part in baseball. Yet, he is still believed by many to be the father

9

of the American sport. So, we are calling the surprising reflections of the divine the in all thing's baseball — the unique relation between our Catholic Faith and the sport which emerged — the Doubleday Code. Let's start to unravel the "Doubleday Code," as we draw analogies between the sport we love, baseball, and the Faith we embrace, Catholicism.

Many have taken baseball for a, or made it their personal, belief system. For example, way back when, Bill Klem, known as the father of baseball umpires, said, "Baseball is more than a game to me, it's a religion." The Hall of Famer, whose career calling balls and strikes spanned five decades, understood baseball's grip on the human mind and heart.

Major League Baseball is similar to religious experience, because it offers fans mystery — the visible with the invisible. Blazing speeds, graceful fielding, split-second timing, blistering hitting, and furious base running occurs amidst the ever-changing unseen strategies, situations, signs, and substitutions. One pitch builds on another; one out on another, one inning on another; and one game on another. There is a lot to take in when watching and contemplating a ball game.

The intelligent fan sees beyond the game's simple objectives to the layers of details, nuances, and complexities. Watching players who perform with wit, skill, and courage at the highest level satisfies our hearts and minds' yearnings to witness nobility in action. That's why we can "religiously" follow the sport. It speaks to our soul, especially if we engage the unfolding drama of each contest with eyes, ears, mind, and heart.

Klem's nearly religious devotion to baseball reflects an ancient relationship between athletic endeavor and values embraced by society. For example, the ancient Greeks considered sport a civic and moral undertaking. Saint Paul, writing to Timothy in the New Testament, elaborates about finishing the race and not for a crown that perishes (2 Tm 4:6–7). (Paul was a Hellenized Jew intimately familiar with the Greek culture). Too bad Paul did not witness a Major League game or enjoy an entire season! He may have advanced a "Catholic theology of the diamond" far beyond Bill Klem's understanding.

Now, if Paul were to write a letter to the Church in America, he might exhort the faithful captivated with the national pastime to look deeper into the mysteries of their own divine calling through their reflections on the game.

He would remind us that, starting with the call of Abraham, God chose a people to be uniquely his own. God sent Abraham to the promised land where many stars of the game emerged to bring the world its first monotheistic religion.

Almost two thousand years later, in fulfillment of his promise to Abraham and the prophets, God sent his only Son. Then, in the fullness of time, Jesus established his Church on the teaching of his apostles to whom he handed on the fullness of the Faith in the Catholic Church. The apostles, of whom Paul says he was the least worthy, spread the good news of salvation to all the nations.

So here we are, two thousand years after Paul preached the Gospel to the Gentiles, witnessing the cultural (and religious) impact of modern professional sports. What does the Father want for us? Could it be that God has chosen a game to be uniquely his own? Could it be that, like the infant beginnings of the Divine Revelation in a tiny Middle Eastern country, a sport developed in America would reflect the fullness of competition at its finest? That this sport would then lead the spiritually-minded fan to ponder eternal truths and see what is hidden right before our eyes?

That's been my experience — a rewarding one — out of which the inspiration for this book comes.

It is folly to think that the origin, growth, and development of the universe and modern baseball somehow evolved from the proverbial primordial soup. On the contrary, both are the product of a loving Father who cares for and sustains all things according to his merciful plan for each of his children.

The fact is the origins of baseball are almost as mysterious, colorful, and complex as the journey of God's chosen people. The call of Abraham, Isaac, Jacob, Moses, David, Solomon were no accidents. Similarly, guided by Divine Providence, baseball developed over a period of decades through the hands of its own patriarchs and prophets: Alexander Cartwright, Alexander Joy, Henry Chadwick, Christy Mathewson, Cy Young, and Cornelius McGillicuddy (Connie Mack), to name a few.

In fact, Doubleday can be likened to Melchizedek, King of Salem, who appears in Genesis. We know not from where Melchizedek comes or where he goes. He blesses Abram who becomes Abraham, our father in faith, from whose lineage the Savior of the world is born.

In like manner, Doubleday appears in baseball lore and then leaves his spirit on the game and his name on the ball field in Cooperstown. A tradition has been handed down to us. I would argue that it's part of God's plan.

Many may scoff and ask why our heavenly Father would trifle with a mere game. But the question to true believers might be, why wouldn't he? Jesus said, "Even the hairs of your head are numbered" (Mt 10:30). God is intimately involved in ALL the affairs of his children. The parables in Scripture illustrate this powerfully when Jesus uses the natural to explain the supernatural. A wedding, a mustard seed, a mill stone, a foundation, a vineyard: all these common things from everyday life provide opportunities for Jesus to explain the mysteries of the Kingdom. Nothing in the sphere of human activity is beyond God's loving gaze. In this sense, even the modern-day game of baseball can lead us to contemplate our final end and God's tender love. In fact, there are so many correspondences between baseball and our spiritual lives that it's hard for me to resist the notion that the game was divinely ordained as a means of teaching spiritual lessons. If we look with the eyes of faith, the mysteries of the supernatural unfold right before our eyes when we *take in a game*.

That millions and millions of fans derive so much joy from such long-playing seasons testifies to baseball's grip on the human intellect and spirit.

As fans, let's not stop at baseball being an end in itself; that would make the "religion" of baseball a form of idolatry. Our love of baseball assumes its rightful place when we understand how it speaks to our spiritual nature. It should call forth our understanding that God made every person in his image with an eternal destiny.

As Saint Augustine put it, "You have made us for yourself, O Lord, and our hearts are restless until they rest in you."

Our purpose in life then is to know, love, and serve God so that we can be happy with him forever in heaven. What should be clear to the serious baseball student and committed Catholic is that the hand of Divine Providence guided it all!

Consider that Major League Baseball is where the game is played the best: skills, depth, majesty, elegance, complexity, all on display. There are other forms of the game, but they are inferior.

Likewise, by the plan of God, the one, holy, apostolic and catholic Church is where the fullness of truth is found. The Catholic Church is superior because her founder, Jesus Christ, is God. The Catholic Church, founded on the testimony of the apostles, was God's idea — not a human being's. The beauty, majesty, depth, coherence, elegance, and consistency of Catholic teaching are unparalleled. Through the Church God gives us Christ, his Son, in Word and sacrament — gifts of profound love. Finally, in the Church we learn why we are on earth and where we are going. Saint Jerome, a Doctor of the Church, wrote, "If anyone is outside the Ark of Noah [that is, the Church] he will perish in the overwhelming flood."

In fact, Our Lord's words comparing the Kingdom of heaven to a king who gave a marriage feast for his son may very well apply to baseball. Jesus said in the parable that the guest without the wedding garment should be cast out into the darkness, "For many are called, but few are chosen" (Mt 22:14). If there were a Major League team in Galilee, perhaps Our Lord would have referred to the player without the proper uniform. For truly many seek to attain the exalted status of a Major Leaguer and do not. Many are indeed called, but few are chosen. Now, very few of us mortals will ever don a Major League uniform and be part of the "Big Show." We will never be called Major Leaguers. But we are all called to be saints. Many are called and few are chosen, because so many will not expend the effort required to be spiritual Major Leaguers. May that not be the case with you.

What follows then are nine (the number of every baseball-themed work) meditations. Each explores a facet of the game in the natural order and draws our intellect to Catholic mysteries in the supernatural order. At the end of each meditation four questions are listed for personal reflection. Consider these as four balls: To begin, an "Intentional Walk" draws you to first base, which represents the virtue of faith. Then you will move toward second base, which represents hope. Finally, you will advance to third base, which is love. These are the theological virtues without which crossing home is impossible. But it starts with faith, so ask the Father for this gift and head to first.

In this way it is hoped that our love for the game leads to a greater love of God, and that the reader is drawn into a deeper relationship with Christ and sets out to seriously run the base paths of faith, hope, and charity to holiness.

Our election to the eternal Hall of Fame depends on it.

1ˢᵀ INNING

The Baseball and the Eucharist

I am the bread of life. — John 6:35

Believe it or not, the "Doubleday Ball" was the first artifact donated to the Cooperstown Baseball Hall of Fame when it opened in 1939, during the celebration of the sport's centennial.

The story goes that Stephen C. Clark, a wealthy Cooperstown local, bought the soiled and torn artifact from a nearby farmer. Allegedly, Clark paid $5 for the ball, which the farmer claimed he found in a trunk in his attic that belonged to Abner Graves.

Graves was a Cooperstown youth who became a gold rush mining engineer in Colorado. Graves' letter, published in the Akron Beacon Journal in 1905, detailed how he (who would have been five years old at the time) was in Cooperstown in 1839 when Doubleday marked off the diamond and set down the rules for this new game called baseball. Based on this flimsy evidence, Clark declared the ball to be the one Doubleday used in the first game. Thus the Doubleday genesis story began. Clark also happened to be the brain thrust behind the Hall of Fame in the bucolic, upstate New York town. And, of course, the ball is on display, or in its archives (the Hall rotates exhibits).

For fans, baseballs used in the Major Leagues, particularly when in play during landmark events or signed by iconic players, have always been hallowed treasures.

Not long ago, Albert Pujols hit a solo home run against the Tigers in Detroit in May 2019. It was a solo shot that put Pujols in an elite club: He joined Hank Aaron and Alex Rodriguez as the third player to reach 2,000 career RBIs. A Tiger fan retrieved the ball in the stands and was immediately approached by Tiger personnel and asked to surrender the ball. He would not.

Negotiating didn't work, either, and the fan kept the ball. When the news went public, the fan was subjected to the modern phenomenon of social-media criticism.

The next day he offered the historic ball to Pujols, but Albert graciously declined, saying fans have a right to keep balls caught at games. Turning down tidy offers for the souvenir, the fan donated the ball three months later to the Hall of Fame. The gift was in memory of his son who died suddenly at twenty-one months old in 2018.

Clark's donation and the Tiger fan's touching gesture to the Major League shrine proves that baseball's essence is, well, the baseball. The small white object without which nothing else in the game matters. It is like the sun in the solar system around which everything else revolves. Every pitch, strike, ball, out, hit, and run involves the ball. Stadiums, bases, bats, gloves, even the players themselves are rendered useless without it. The baseball defines the game. No ball, no game.

The importance and reverence imparted to the ball by baseball powers cannot be overstated. There are very stringent requirements for both its construction and the use of the ball in play. Major League Baseball's (MLB) balls are handmade to exacting standards at the Rawlings Sporting Goods facility in Costa Rica. Each ball is 9 to 9¼" in circumference and weighs 5 to 5¼ ounces. Only a cowhide cover is used in construction and 108 double stitches are placed in each ball by hand.

Once sent to the ballpark the ball undergoes more treatment. MLB specifically requires that umpires rub each ball with Lena Blackburne's Rubbing Mud (the composition of the mud is a guarded secret). This treatment takes the slickness and sheen off the pristine cowhide leather without besmirching the white surface. Once the ball preparation has been religiously observed, it is ready for play.

In the confines of stadiums everywhere, the game begins with the home plate umpire crying out, "Play Ball!" That cues the pitcher to launch his first pitch, and the confined universe of a baseball game goes into motion. Each ball is different; each ball is the same. A total of 120 to 150 balls are used in the course of a nine-inning game. The seemingly endless supply testifies to the meticulous attention paid to the ball and its condition. Great care is taken to have a pristine ball in play at all times. One touch with the dirt, grass, or wall and the ball is taken out of play. A dirty ball could distort the batter's vision; a scuffed or nicked ball could be used to the pitcher's advantage. Only the best is in play.

Almost all played balls will end up in the stands, grabbed by fans eager to possess the souvenir — to take part of the game home with them. In fact, the ubiquitous baseball is sought after by every fan that ever attended a game. Autographed baseballs are valued and revered in display cases, sold at auctions and sought by collectors. Nothing in baseball is more sacrosanct than the ball.

No wonder Stephen C. Clark gave up Doubleday's soiled ball and the Tiger fan offered up the Pujols ball for veneration!

Now, let's look deeper into this Doubleday mystery fueled by the first ball in Cooperstown. Just as the small white object is the consuming reference for all things baseball, there is a parallel in the Catholic Church. IT IS THE EUCHARIST.

The endless supply of baseballs at Major League games should direct our thoughts to the multiplication of the loaves. Like a Major League game's supply of baseballs, the bread Our Lord feeds His fans is never exhausted. He provided food for the 5,000 with five loaves (see Jn 6) and fed the 4,000 with seven loaves (Mk 8). These miracles show what Divine power can do with bread. By the multiplication of the loaves, Our Lord anticipated the Eucharist and had in mind how he would feed all fans that would be members of his team. Jesus said this explicitly, "The bread that I will give is my flesh for the life of the world" (Jn 6:51).

Every Catholic Christian should see clearly that just as the baseball defines the game and is its source, so the Eucharist defines the Church. The *Catechism of the Catholic Church* states clearly: "The Eucharist is 'the source and summit of the Christian life.' The other sacraments, and indeed all ecclesiastical ministries and works of apostolate, are bound up with the Eucharist and are oriented toward it. For in the blessed Eucharist is contained the whole spiritual good of the Church, namely Christ himself, our Pasch" (1324). If there is one word to describe the Catholic Church it is "Eucharist," for without Christ himself nothing else matters. The source and summit of our spiritual life, therefore, demands great care and excellence.

So it is that the host (like the baseball) is made with exacting requirements according to Catholic liturgical norms, containing only the finest wheat flour and purest water. The host is essential for the Eucharistic celebration of the holy sacrifice of the Mass. It is there that the small white host is elevated along with the chalice containing the wine becomes truly the body and blood of Christ — the source and summit of Christian life!

Furthermore, the Eucharist, as the source and summit of the Faith, is like the sun in the solar system around which all the sacraments and teachings of the Church revolve. This gift of the body and blood of our blessed Lord is given to us through the holy sacrifice of the Mass. It was at the Last Supper, the first Mass, that Jesus conferred on his priests this incredible power to change bread into his body and wine into his blood. This change is called "transubstantiation," because in the Mass the host (bread) and the wine are changed into *the very flesh and blood of Christ*. Only the accidents of appearance remain, but the substance is *the very flesh and blood Christ*. Yes, this fact merits my purposeful repetition.

By receiving Our Lord with love we become more like him, and this personal relationship with him through the Eucharist is the greatest gift God the Father can bestow in this life as preparation for the next. Jesus says to us, "Truly, truly, I say to you, unless you eat the flesh of the Son of Man and drink his blood, you have no life within you; he who eats my flesh and drinks my blood has eternal life, and I will raise him up on the last day" (Jn 6:53–54). Without Christ, not much else in the game of life matters: the Bible, the dogma, the liturgy, even the priesthood and papacy are rendered ineffective without the Eucharist. No ball, no game. No Eucharist, no Christ.

But this doctrine is one of the most challenging to grasp. We see this vividly when Jesus announced that he is the Bread of Life and told his followers that they must literally *eat his flesh and drink his blood*. Notice the reaction of the disciples recorded in the Gospel. The Jews quarreled among themselves saying, "How can this man give us his flesh to eat?" (Jn 6:52). And another reaction: Many of his disciples who were listening said, "this is a hard saying; who can listen to it?" (Jn 6:60). Finally, John records the result of this rejection of Our Lord's teaching. Many of his disciples returned to their former way of life and no longer accompanied him (see Jn 6:66).

We see the response of many of Christ's followers to this sublime teaching, all because of the faith asked of them. It is here that Judas first failed the test of discipleship. Jesus points this out, "'Did I not choose you the twelve, and one of you is a devil?' He spoke of Judas, son of Simon the Iscariot, for he, one of the twelve, would betray him" (Jn 6:70–71). Thus it is that Judas failed the great Eucharistic test because of the faith that was asked of him.

To close this meditation, imagine going to a Major League stadium and there seeing the fans, vendors, players, pristine-groomed field, and teams in their crisp uniforms — but there were no baseballs! How disappointing and futile the event would be without the source and summit of the game. Draw the correct conclusion. It is the same in Christian churches without the Eucharist. No ball, no game. No Eucharist, no Christ.

Oh, the love of God who condescended to make himself so approachable. He made the common elements of our earthy life, bread and wine, true spiritual food for all in his Church. The Catholic baseball fan sees this preeminent mystery and appreciates and loves attending the Mass, more than he would the seventh game of the World Series.

A final point by way of admonition: Just as the pitcher is always offering an immaculate baseball to the batter, so Christ offers us the purest and holiest Host. The one who receives such a gift must be in the state of grace or free from serious sin to receive him. To receive Our Lord in a state of sin is a sacrilege — far worse than the "Black Sox" purposely losing the World Series in 1919. A sacrilege means spiritual death if not forgiven in confession. Saint Paul explains it thus: "Whoever, therefore, eats the bread or drinks the cup of the Lord in an unworthy manner will be guilty of profaning the body and blood of the Lord" (1 Cor 11:27). A good confession to a priest is the means to predispose our soul to embrace our Eucharistic Lord.

This first analogy between the Eucharist and the baseball is only the start of how reflections on baseball can focus our attention on the divine mysteries.

—

QUESTIONS FOR REFLECTION - THE INTENTIONAL WALK

⚾ BALL ONE

Read John chapter 6. Some say the Eucharist is a symbol of Christ's body and blood. Do I think the disciples would abandon Christ if it were just a symbol that Christ spoke about?

⚾ BALL TWO

"He who eats my flesh and drinks my blood abides in me, and I in him" (Jn 6:56). Our Catholic Faith should deepen and confirm our faith in Christ's words. Do I desire to have Christ live in me and I in him?

⚾ BALL THREE

What kind of preparation do I make before receiving Christ in holy Communion? Am I in the state of grace, conscious of no serious unconfessed sin on my soul?

⚾ BALL FOUR

Am I willing to share enthusiastically my belief and love for Christ in the Eucharist with others? Do I visit him often in church where he is present, body, blood, soul, and divinity, to return his tender love for me?

—ON DECK—

St. Thérèse of Lisieux (*HOF*)

"He does not come down from heaven each day to stay in a gold chalice. He comes down to find another heaven he cherishes infinitely more than the first, the heaven of our souls made in his image, living temples of the most Blessed Trinity!"

2ᴺᴰ INNING

Nine-Inning Nervous Breakdown and the Drama of the Mass

I have earnestly desired to eat this passover with you before I suffer.
— Luke 22:15

"Baseball is boring. It is nine minutes of action crowded into 3 hours." That's what an Irish priest (a true spiritual father) told me when I tried to explain why Major League Baseball must be God's favorite sport. Father was a soccer fan and actually a very good player.

I responded: "Father, isn't that what many Catholics say about the Mass? 'The Mass is boring,' they say. 'I don't get anything out of the Mass.'"

Then I followed up building on a quote from St. Jose María Escrivá de Balaguer; I told my soccer-saturated padre that if you think baseball or the Mass is boring it's "because your senses are awake and your soul is asleep." You really need to know the finer points of both to experience the depth and richness of each. In fact, Leo Durocher said it best: "Baseball is like church. Many attend: few understand." Correct on both accounts.

Baseball is an incredible sport. To the serious fan the blaring music, mascot races, and kiss cams are a distraction and often not appreciated by baseball purists. That stuff is a concession to the lazy fan and the culture of instant gratification where the senses must be assaulted at every moment to stave off other distractions.

Baseball makes demands on the fan to be attentive, observant, and thoughtful. To quote Hall of Fame announcer Red Barber: "Baseball is dull only to dull minds." A nine-inning nervous breakdown is how the television ads promotes the Major League Baseball playoffs.

Mass in the Catholic Church is misunderstood and unappreciated on a whole other level. Many, if not most, of the faithful seek out slick homilies (not necessarily a profound explication of the mysteries of revelation), a charismatic priest, and accomplished choral singing (or guitar "worship teams"). Some even spend their time anticipating the doughnut klatches after Mass and the fellowship they supply. There are no words to describe how breathtakingly shallow these attitudes are. It is a tragedy of epic proportions that may even be lost on the clergy, as well as the lay faithful in the pews.

To put this lack of understanding of the Mass into perspective I offer a quote from the stigmatic priest Saint Padre Pio: "It would be easier for the world to survive without the sun than to do without holy Mass." Stop and think about that. Without the **sun** there is no earthly existence — no life on the planet. Saint Pio's point is that without the **Son**'s death on the cross there is no point in life. Eternity vanishes as well. Stop and really ponder that.

Back to baseball before we take up the sublime topic of the Mass. Major League Baseball is played over days, weeks, and months. Often the pennant race or playoff spot turns on one victory. Over the course of a 162-game season a team will lose several close games where one hanging curve, one at bat or one throw is the difference between victory and defeat. On the mound, at the plate, in the field, and the dugout there is a lot going on at once. And it is all about runs — either moving runners and scoring, or preventing base runners and getting outs. Baseball is exciting because no matter how badly a team is losing it can come back. There is no clock to run out. There is always enough time because the opposition has to get the outs. And often the most difficult outs to get occur during the last three innings. As Dizzy Dean once remarked after a 1-0 game, "The game was closer than the score indicated."

Some examples of how a game can turn: take game four of the World Series in 1941 — the year of Joe DiMaggio's 56-game hitting streak. The Yankees were up two games to one playing at Ebbets Field. The Dodgers entered the ninth with a 4-3 lead with imposing Hugh Carey on the mound. He promptly retired the first two Yankees and worked the count to 3-and-2 to Tommy Henrich. The payoff pitch was a swing and a miss for strike three — GAME OVER. NO. Dodger catcher Mickey Owens missed the ball and Heinrich reached first base safely. That was the catcher's first error in a year! After that, DiMaggio, Charlie Keller, Bill Dickey, Joe Gordon, and Phil Rizzuto reached base in succession. The Yankees came back for a 7-4 victory and won the series the next day.

Another series victory evaporated in one play in 2011 when the Cardinals were down to the last strike against the Texas Rangers. Taking a two-run lead into the bottom of the ninth, David Freese stepped to the plate with two on and two out. With two strikes, Freese launched a fly to right over Nelson Cruz's head. Every astute baseball fan anticipated Cruz, who was playing deep to guard against an extra-base hit, would track down the ball for the final out and a never-to-be-forgotten end to the Rangers long history of losing. The ball kept carrying, though, and turned into a triple off the wall. No way should a ball hit the wall within reach of the fielder's glove in that situation — two out in the last inning! It happened, though, which tied the game. The Cardinals went on to win in extra innings on another long ball by Freese, this one a homer. Like the '41 Yankees, the Cardinals closed out the series the next day. Think nine-inning nervous breakdown — especially when you see the reaction of the fans to ebb and flow of pitch counts, outs, and runs.

Finally, Game Seven in the 1968 World Series between the Cardinals and Tigers in Detroit turned into a pitchers' duel between Bob Gibson and Mickey Lolich. That year became known as the "year of the pitcher." Bob Gibson established the all-time record low ERA for a pitcher at 1.12. Lolich's teammate Denny McClain won 30 games that year. To say the least, runs were hard to come by — so hard that the height of Major League pitching mounds was lowered the next year to give hitters a fighting chance.

The score remained 0-0 heading into the bottom of the sixth inning when Lou Brock led off with a single. Everyone expected Brock to steal — despite being held on by lefty Lolich with a good move to first. Brock drew the throw to first, and first baseman Norm Cash nailed Brock at second. Cardinal fans shouted, "No!" How could the best base stealer in history to that point get pick off as the lead runner in a scoreless contest! Brock was rarely, if ever, picked off.

The next Cardinal batter, Julian Javier, lined out. That brought up Curt Flood, who singled to deep short. The speedy Flood was *also promptly picked off by Lolich*. No runs, two hits, no errors, none left on for the Cardinals. If Brock had played it safe, Flood's single would have put a man on first and second with one out. But, no-o-o-o-o!

The Tigers went on to score three in the seventh and won 4-1. Lolich hurled a complete game victory, his third of the series, pitching on short rest. Those pitches he didn't have to throw in the sixth were huge. The fan understands this as it's happening. Every true baseball fan practically has a pitch count running in his head, and understands the longer each inning — even an at bat — the better chance there is a pitcher's stuff will eventually fail. That's why, to the true fan, a batter fouling off pitch after pitch, extending his at bat, keeps improving his odds of getting a hit himself and for the batters coming up behind him. Even long pitch counts are enthralling for those who know the ins and outs of a single at bat.

An astute and knowledgeable fan does not become that way over night. It takes time, effort (although very enjoyable effort), and some study. But the end result is extremely rewarding. The connection to one's favorite team almost becomes like an extension of the family. There are so many memories of thrill-filled victories and inevitably agonizing defeats.

Just ask any rabid Phillies fan over the age of sixty-five about the team's collapse the last week of the 1964 season (to this day known as the PHOLD). I was ten years old and still remember my tears when I realized the Phillies were not going to play the Yankees in the World Series. The Phils had a six-and-a-half game lead in late September, only to lose ten straight games and blow the pennant.

The collapse started with a 1-0 loss to the Reds when Chico Ruiz stole home with Frank Robinson at bat. Slugger Robinson was probably the most surprised person on the planet at that moment. I'll bet if Ruiz had been caught stealing Robinson would have had an interesting reaction to the foolhardy play. But that is the beauty of baseball. Many games are won in totally unexpected ways. The players are so good, the competitors so evenly matched, that it takes somebody executing above and beyond his normal level (execution of the most basic plays in Major League Baseball is done at such a high level that most fans — as one Major Leaguer remarked — wouldn't even be able to catch routine throws from the infield to first base). Last place teams beat first place teams, and sometimes even cellar dwellers knock contenders out of a pennant race. A 1-0 game in which the pitching is superb is every bit as gut wrenching as a 10-9 fireworks show.

A Major League game is somewhat like the liturgy in that you must see the unseen; the consequence one action has upon another. You have to know the players and their tendencies. Taking in a game means looking back to what happened in past innings as well as looking ahead in the batter order. Astute fans think along with the manager, second-guessing decisions and anticipating the next move. The fan thinks about the situation and how it should be played. Put on the hit-and-run? Give a batter the green light on a 3-0 pitch? Sacrifice or swing away? While these calculations are being made, the fury of the batter-pitcher confrontation continues with no letup. Nine innings can often change the trajectory of a season or a career. Baseball is not boring.

In fact, any endeavor that demands knowledge and skill — be it music, math, science, art, politics, poetry, and especially marriage and faith — is only boring if "our senses are awake and our soul is asleep."

Now, the key takeaway is that a Catholic who appreciates the deeper levels of Major League Baseball should be especially capable of appreciating the liturgy on a deeper level as well. As most baseball fans do not understand the deeper and most significant elements of the game, so most Catholics do not understand fully the enormity of the Sacred Liturgy. It, too, takes time, effort, and study. To properly offer Mass — not just attend — you must understand the players, the action, and the elements. You must be able to see the unseen and comprehend the lofty mysteries of God's love contained in the drama. Let's explore the mystery of the Mass by answering a few questions.

First, why is the Mass so important? Why would Saint Padre Pio state that it is "more important than the sun"?

The Church, through the Bible, offers a clear and concise explanation. Lucifer (meaning light-bearer) rebelled against God and was expelled from heaven introducing discord into God's harmony of creation. Because of his superior angelic intellect and attributes, Lucifer was not given a second chance. He understood the consequences of his rebellion and exercised his free will; therefore, his rupture in relationship with God was final and eternal.

Our first parents were not angelic beings but humans. God gave them free will as well, and allowed them to exercise that gift in the garden. Adam and Eve fell into sin but did not realize the enormity of their act. In fact, they thought they could hide their sin from their Creator by sewing fig leaves. As a consequence of sin, God banished Adam and Eve and, consequently, the human race from paradise (yes, the Church teaches that Adam and Eve were really our first parents and not fictional characters in the story). But in his tender love, God promised to send a redeemer. In other words, Adam and Eve and all the children to follow were given a second chance. The gates to paradise were once barred forever, but the gates of heaven would be opened again.

Hence, the human race was commanded by God to bear

children in the hopes that one born of woman would reverse the effects of sin. That was the reason — God's plan — for the continuation of the human race. It follows that Christ's death on the cross, then, is the most important event in history. It is through the passion, death, and resurrection of our blessed Lord that we are saved. No other way. And the Mass is the re-presentation of the passion, death, and resurrection of Christ to the Father. The Mass is the very same sacrifice of Calvary offered to the Father on our behalf. That is why the Sacred Liturgy is more important than the sun. Who needs the sun or this planet if there is no hope of eternal happiness? Think about this deeply.

What is the sacrifice of the Mass? And why is missing Mass on Sunday a mortal sin?

Jesus, at the Last Supper on the night before he died, told his apostles more than once, "If you love me, keep my commandments." The first commandment is to not have other gods. The third is to keep the Lord's day holy. We honor both commandments by attending Mass as it is the perfect prayer offered in union with Christ's sacrifice for our sins and victory over death.

Read the *Catechism*'s explanation of the Mass in Part Two, "The Celebration of the Christian Mystery." "The Eucharist is thus a sacrifice because it *re-presents* (make present) the sacrifice of the cross" (1366). The Mass is the re-presentation of Christ's death on the cross offered in an unbloody manner. It is not another sacrifice or a different sacrifice, but the same one. On Calvary, Jesus was both priest and victim offering himself to the Father as a satisfaction for sins. Christ was both priest and victim. In the Mass, the very same body and blood of Christ are offered to the eternal Father in expiation for sin in an unbloody manner. In the Mass, Christ is the victim who offers himself through the words and actions of the priest. The Mass then is Calvary made present to us. This is the teaching of the Church for two thousand years as handed down by the apostles, who were given the command by Christ to "do this in remembrance of me" (Lk 21:19).

What happens at the Mass? What is the deeper meaning of what takes place before our eyes?

Just as the stadium is the place of drama, so, too, Catholic churches are the scene of the eternal drama. On each altar, every day, at all hours of the day, somewhere in the world a Catholic Mass is being offered. Remember, there is a difference between taking in a ball game, being imaginatively involved in the drama, and merely watching one, just as there is a huge difference in attending Mass and participating in

BASEBALL INNINGS	ORDER OF THE MASS
First	Sign of the Cross and Penitential Rite
Second	Gloria and the Collect or Opening Prayer
Third	Liturgy of the Word
Fourth	Homily
Fifth	Profession of Faith — Creed
Sixth	Offertory
Seventh	Consecration
Eighth	Communion
Ninth	Blessing and Dismissal

offering the sublime gift of Christ and ourselves to the Father. To complete the parallel between the ball game and the liturgy we will break the liturgy down into nine distinct actions (as in the table on page 32) and then begin to explain the drama as it unfolds.

Like the first pitch, the Mass always begins with the Sign of the Cross, bringing together two central mysteries of the Faith. Through this action, we invoke the Blessed Trinity, adoring the Father, Son and Holy Spirit, while calling to mind the cross' significance in reconciling us to this Triune God.

Next the priest recites a short phrase of Scripture, known as the Entrance Antiphon, calling the faithful to worship.

Nearly instantaneously, in the "first inning," we call to mind our sins and ask forgiveness — either through reciting the prayer of general confession or singing the *Kyrie Eleison* (sometimes the prayer of general confession is followed by the *Kyrie Eleison*). Here all venial sin is taken away; perfect preparation for the life-giving events that are anticipated to come in the later innings.

During non-penitential seasons — that is, outside of Lent and Advent — the *Gloria* follows, which is the preeminent prayer of worship and praise to the Trinity, acknowledging the Divine's sublime attributes.

Next is the Collect (opening prayer), offered to our loving Triune God, which expresses the intentions and supplications of the Church and those in our individual hearts.

The first third of the liturgy concludes with the Liturgy of the Word: readings from the Old Testament, the Psalms, the New Testament, and the Gospel. If one listens intently, as if hearing the passage for the first time, the heart and mind are sure to open in faith to God's love. God will speak to us, move our hearts, enlighten our minds, and vivify our spirits. This is a fruit of true faith and effort, not the fruit of an emotional high. Like hitting, it takes practice, patience and concentration to grow in faith, hope, and charity through the word of God. The work of perfection is more in God's hands than ours, but we must come prepared to see and hear, as we resolve to act in accordance to what we've come to understand.

Christ is truly present in his Word. He lives in us, acts through us, and loves us through his Word. To respond in kind to this love may be difficult, demanding a change in our lives of which we feel incapable, but it can hardly be boring. We find ourselves in the presence of the Almighty God, a God who is a jealous God, who invites us to enter into his divine life. We should now be especially cognizant of the ever-present drama of God's outreach to us.

Having made it through the batting order the first time, the next three innings showcase the homily, profession of faith and prayers of the faithful. We might wish to imagine that the priest (or deacon) is like the pitcher who takes the mound to fire the pitches of the prophets and evangelists at the wiles of the infernal enemy, the devil. Here we are in the field playing our positions, ready to swallow up grounders, spear line drives, and track down the fly balls that come our way. In other words, we play defense against the world, the flesh and the devil.

A good pitcher — or homilist — will help the team retire the side, but some pitching is weak and requires heroic plays in the field. Here we equip ourselves as best we can to contribute to the team, to understand and live the word of God. Note here one more baseball parallel: Great preachers, like great pitchers, are a rare commodity. The pitcher is part of the game but not the game. If we focus solely on the priest and the homily for satisfaction and value, we are badly misled. The best is yet to come, when Christ himself enters the game again.

The middle innings conclude with the Creed and the prayers of the faithful before coming to the offertory. The basis of the Creed was actually given to us by the apostles, but we recite the Nicene Creed formulated at the Council of Nicaea which was held in AD 325 and presided over by Emperor Constantine. It is a compelling statement of the nonnegotiable truths of the Faith. Recite it with attention and tenacity.

We follow with the prayers of the faithful because Jesus

himself told us: "Ask, and it will be given to you; seek and you will find" (Mt 7:7). Thus we pray for the Church, civic leaders, our country and the world, and our own intentions in our families and personal lives. Make this plate appearance count. Things are about to get exciting.

Heading into the final few innings, we come to the Liturgy of the Eucharist: offertory, consecration, and Communion. These three parts of the Mass make present the Last Supper, the Crucifixion, and the Resurrection. It is here that we can, in the words of Yogi Berra to his players, "observe a lot by just watching." Like baseball, there is a lot to see and experience at the apex of the drama we call the Mass. It is thrilling, engaging and life changing as long as our senses and **soul** are awake.

The offertory begins with bread and wine, recalling for us the Last Supper. These two substances must be used to have a valid Mass. Why? First, because our blessed Lord used these for the first consecration. Second, each nourish the human race and by offering what gives us our physical substance we offer ourselves. And third, Archbishop Fulton Sheen explained that each of the elements must undergo crucifixion: wheat must be ground in a mill and grapes crushed in a press to become what they are. As the many grains of wheat that make up the host and the many grapes constitute the wine, each represent the unity of the members of the Church brought together for the sacrifice.

So we are on the altar! Through the bread and wine that will become the Body of Christ our lives, gifts, and talents are placed on the paten and in the chalice. Notice further that the priest will take a tiny bit of water and put it in the chalice with the wine. Wine has color, taste, fragrance, and potency. Water is colorless, odorless, tasteless, and without potency. Wine represents divinity and water our humanity.

Pay special attention to the prayer offered as the water is poured: "By the mystery of this water and wine may we come to share in the divinity of Christ who humbled himself to share in our humanity." We are not only on the altar, but a change is coming — we are being, little by little at each Mass, transformed into another Christ!

Before we go into the next few innings it is crucial that we grasp one fact about the majesty of being a spiritual Major Leaguer. By our baptism we share the grace of the indwelling of the Holy Trinity in our souls. God himself is present in us if, by grace, we live a life of grace, refraining from rejecting God by mortal sin. In other words, we possess the Holy Trinity in our souls in a mysterious way, and that is where all our concentration should be. God is not up there somewhere. He loves us personally and individually in the here and now. Jesus tells us, "If a man loves me, he will keep my word, and my Father will love him, and we will come and make our home with him" (Jn 14:23).

The Last Supper offering now moves to Calvary. The gifts are prepared, and it is the solemn moment of consecration. The priest stands in the place of Christ (*in persona Christi*) so that Christ can change the bread and wine into his **flesh** and **blood**.

For when the priest pronounces the words of consecration, "This is my body" and "This is my blood," the elements' substance is changed. Christ, the eternal High Priest makes Calvary present.

Notice closely how this happens. The priest first raises the host and says, "This is my body," then the chalice, "This is my blood." The separate consecration presents the reality of Christ truly hanging on the cross. It is as if the very cross holding the pierced Body of Christ is lifted out of the rocks in Jerusalem and transported 2000 years and placed on our altar. We are present at the very same sacrifice of Christ on the cross — in an unbloody manner. Same priest, same victim, same sacrifice.

Now recall that at the offertory we placed ourselves on the paten and in the chalice: The bread and wine represent us. What can this mean and how does it affect us?

Stop and consider that Christ had no reason to die for himself. He died for us. He died to take our human nature and transform it into his divine nature. So, then, if we placed ourselves on the altar at the offertory, we are now incorporated into Christ's death at the consecration. The bread is no longer bread but the flesh of Christ. The wine is no longer wine but the blood of Christ. And in both we offer to the Father our human, sinful, finite existence so that we may die with Christ to our sinfulness and become ever more like him. Each and every Mass we offer with attention and devotion effects a change in us and advances us along the base paths of the virtues of faith and charity — gifts that only come to us from God. Make your offering pleasing to the Father by praying with intensity and devotion.

Do you see the holy exchange taking place? We die with Christ to our sinfulness. We are with Christ at Calvary, as he takes his sins upon us. His passion provides forgiveness for our sins by putting them to death through the sacrifice of his own life.

Now we come to Communion. Recall that in the offertory we offered ourselves to Christ in an act of radical identification. Therefore, we die with Christ at the consecration — the moment when flesh and blood as represented by bread and wine is transformed into his body and blood. By the reception of his body and blood in holy Communion we will receive Christ's life into our own.

Again, we must "observe a lot by watching." The Our Father is recited while Christ is on the cross. Christ's sacrifice is the supreme example of the Father's will being done on earth as it is in heaven. Here, we enter into the eternal reality of Christ's atonement — his sacrifice that becomes present again at each Mass. He is slain, and our old life of sin put to death, in the unbloody sacrifice of the Mass.

Next is the sacrifice and resurrection! A most exciting finish.

There can be no sacrifice unless the victim is immolated, in other words, sacrificed. Notice carefully that at the recitation of the *Agnus Dei* the priest breaks the Host! The Host is the living body of Jesus on the altar. So here the breaking of the host is the sacrifice of Christ ... the tearing of his flesh. My God, how I love thee!

Watch what happens next; the priest breaks off a particle of

Christ's body and places it in the chalice, uniting body and blood. Now, if the separate consecration of body and blood earlier in the Mass represent death, here the uniting of body and blood represents life. It is real. It is not the dead Jesus from the cross that we receive. It is the risen Jesus who feeds us the substance of his flesh and blood to complete our incorporation into his mystical body, the Church; his physical body for strength in life's journey; and his divinity to transform us into his nature for heaven.

Like a hitter on deck, we should be preparing our mind hearts and bodies for the moment we receive the Divine Guest. And the moments following the reception of holy Communion should be most precious to us. We should, if we exercise faith, be lost in praise and thanksgiving speaking to Our Lord of all that we need and desire. We should ask him for the graces to live a holy life and die a holy death and to imitate him in doing the will of the Father. Ask yourself: Are my senses awake to divine reality of receiving the holy Eucharist? Is my soul awake in anticipation and love? If so, the Mass is never boring. And you never leave early!

Jesus said to his apostles at the Last Supper, "I have earnestly desired to eat this passover with you before I suffer" (Lk 22:15). It is the only time in the Gospel Jesus expresses his desire to do anything. If he could have given us anything better, he would have done it!

Now, the last inning is three up and three down as we offer thanks and receive God's blessing as new creations in Christ. Christ has won the victory. The game is ours. We are ready to go out to do battle with sin and to love others.

O holy, wonderous, glorious liturgy. Catholics are most blessed. Who needs the sun when you have the *Son*?

Are you now prepared to offer, truly offer with attention and devotion, the holy sacrifice of the Mass? More exciting than any nine-inning nervous breakdown.

QUESTIONS FOR REFLECTION - THE INTENTIONAL WALK

BALL ONE

How seriously do I prepare to participate in the Holy Sacrifice of the Mass? For the reception of the holy Eucharist? For confession?

BALL TWO

What I love I spend much time on: Have I studied the Mass and my faith to have a Major League knowledge to impart to others or is my knowledge at the T-ball level?

BALL THREE

Do I contemplate the mystery of the presence of the Holy Trinity in my soul through the Mass, sacraments, and prayer? Do I thank God every day for the gift of the Mass and holy Eucharist?

BALL FOUR

Do I seek to surrender my will to God at each mass as Jesus did in mounting the cross? Do I ask the Father what he wants of me? Do I listen in silence so that Our Lord can speak to my heart?

—ON DECK—

Saint Padre Pio (*Hall of Fame*)

"If only we knew how God regards this sacrifice, we would risk our lives to be present at a single Mass."

3ᴿᴰ INNING

Baseball and Baptism: The Uniform and the Position

Go into all the world and preach the gospel to the whole creation.
He who believes and is baptized will be saved; but he who does not
believe will be condemned. — Mark 16:15–16

Before I formed you in the womb I knew you. — Jeremiah 1:5

The story I'm about to tell tracks a unique and never-to-be-repeated path that one player traveled to the roster of a Major League team. It's the stuff of novels and Hollywood movies. From the Catholic perspective, it also showcases the mystery of Divine Providence.

On Saturday, May 18, 1912, Aloysius Joseph "Allan" Travers took the mound at Shibe Park (later known as Connie Mack Stadium) and pitched a complete game for the Detroit Tigers. It was his Major League debut and also his final appearance in the Big Show.

Allan never pitched in the minor leagues or anywhere else for that matter. In fact, he played the violin, not baseball. The closest he had ever come to a pitching mound was as student assistant manager for the St. Joseph's College baseball team. He had no plans to ever pitch until fate intervened. That Saturday, he volunteered to pitch for the Tigers to make some extra money — twenty-five dollars to play and an extra twenty-five (by some accounts) if he pitched and finished the game. So, Allan threw and threw and threw, facing fifty Philadelphia Athletics' batters. The Athletics happened to have won the previous year's World Series.

Here is how he got to the mound that divinely appointed day. Three days earlier, the Tigers were playing in New York when

41

a disabled Yankee fan hurled an insult at Ty Cobb. Cobb promptly went into the seats and pummeled the man. American League President Ban Johnson was in attendance and, witnessing Cobb's thuggery, suspended Cobb indefinitely.

Cobb's fellow Tigers immediately retaliated by launching the first baseball strike, walking out for the game in Philadelphia. Johnson then threatened to fine the Tigers $5,000 (a huge sum in those days) for each gamed missed.

A desperate Tiger owner Frank Navin instructed his manager, Hughie Jennings, to find replacements. The story goes that Jennings found Allan, a junior at St. Joseph's College, on a street corner in north Philadelphia. Recruiting other sandlot players hanging around with Travers, Jennings, along with two aging Tiger coaches, took the field, sending Allan to the mound against the mighty Athletics.

The Tigers lost 24-2 and the record book tells a dismal but incomplete story. The twenty-year-old "rookie" pitched eight innings, surrendering twenty-four runs on twenty-six hits, walked seven, and accumulated a career ERA of 15.75. Under normal circumstances an utter failure. But considering the rest of the story, we will see that God writes straight here with the proverbial crooked lines. Allan struck out one batter. Ten of the runs scored against him were unearned because the defense was as proficient as Little League right fielders. He gave up no home runs, including to future Hall of Famers Frank "Home Run" Baker and Eddie Collins. He even had seven assists for a perfect fielding percentage of 1.000.

The performance was good enough for a scout to approach Allan to determine if he had interest in pursuing a career. Here is where God stepped in, though. The following spring, after Allan graduated from St. Joseph's, he entered the Society of Jesus (the Jesuits) and in 1926 was ordained a priest — the only Major Leaguer (even if just for one day) ever to enter this higher calling.

After ordination Allan had the best of both worlds. Forevermore, Allan Travers could say he was a Major Leaguer. The Tiger uniform would place baseball's indelible mark on him as it does for all of those happy few who make an appearance in even one game at a Major League stadium.

Yet, a more sublime consideration is that Allan had received the indelible mark of the Sacrament of Holy Orders. Instead of saving games he would be saving souls. The reception of the Sacraments of Baptism and Confirmation had prepared him for the sublime reception of the Sacrament of Holy Orders. These are the same sacraments that prepare us to pursue our own Major League calling in the Catholic Faith.

The *Catechism of the Catholic Church* explains the beautiful teaching this way:

> The three sacraments of Baptism, Confirmation, and Holy Orders confer, in addition to grace, a sacramental *character* or "seal" by which the Christian shares in Christ's priesthood and is made a member of the Church according to different states and functions. This configuration to Christ and to the Church, brought about by the Spirit, is indelible; it remains forever in the Christian as a positive disposition for grace, a promise and guarantee of divine protection, and as a vocation to divine worship and to the service of the Church. Therefore, these sacraments can never be repeated. (1121)

While Allan Travers' baseball experience is unique, the mystery of his divine calling is not and applies to each us. This is so because, through the Sacrament of Baptism, God puts a Major League uniform on each of us and confers singular graces to play our position and answer his calling to perform at the highest level of virtue. We become temples of the Holy Spirit, meaning the Holy Trinity takes up residence in our souls! Wow.

Do we understand the dignity of our calling that baptism confers on us? Recall how Our Lord was baptized by John at the beginning of his public ministry, thus making all waters holy. Jesus told his apostles: "Go into all the world and preach the gospel to the whole creation. He who believes and is baptized will be saved; but he who does not believe will be condemned" (Mk 16:15–16).

Thus Jesus shows us the divine nature of our calling as Catholics, who by this wondrous sacrament, baptism, have original sin removed and are made children of God. The grace we receive through baptism is the very presence of God in our souls. By baptism we share in the common priesthood of all believers as explained in the *Catechism*. At the outset of our lives as Christians, we are given a "spiritual Major League uniform," as we become the sons and daughters of God. The sacrament confers an indelible mark upon our immortal souls.

When we see the iconic Yankee pinstripes, the White Sox black, Dodger blue, and Cardinal redbird (the color of clerical cardinals in the Church) we should be reminded of our baptism. Going further with the analogy, we can imagine the cap as an offshoot of the Kippah, or yarmulkes (pronounced yamakas), but with the addition of the bill, or bill of Christ, which allows one to play in the presence of the sun (Son) and keep one's eyes focused on home (heaven).

Moreover, as the uniform identifies a player as a member of a team and allows him to step out on the field, so our spiritual uniform identifies us as Christ's own and enables us to take up his mission.

Thousands upon thousands of baseball players never achieve the distinction of donning a Major League uniform. Only the most-skilled players enjoy this lifelong distinction. They have excelled at level after level in the quest for this stellar achievement. Blessed by God with extraordinary talent and physical ability, Divine Providence has seen to it that they are placed in an environment where they can succeed. A National or American League pro will always be able to say, like Allan Travers, "I made the big leagues." The pitcher who tosses only a third of an inning or the journeyman who registers just one at bat is a Major Leaguer in the Baseball Book of Records. He has put on the uniform of a pro and that distinction can never be taken away.

Yes, to wear a Major Leaguer's garb puts someone in rarefied company, considering that on any given day throughout the season only 750 players suit up. For the thousands and thousands of aspiring players at every level Scripture applies: "For many are called but few are chosen" (Mt 22:14). To don a Major League uniform just one time! What a dream come true for the addicted baseball fan. But the call from the Major League office never comes for millions of us. Sometimes all we can do is aspire to just walk on the field at our favorite stadium.

Not so for the Catholic player on our blessed Lord's ball club. The call comes for sure. And we never know where that summons will lead. Again, Al Travers "career" is an example. A priest for forty-two years, Father Travers taught at St. Francis Xavier High School in Manhattan and was later named Dean of Men at St. Joseph College in Philadelphia. From 1943 to 1968, he taught Spanish and religion at Saint Joseph's Preparatory School, also in Philadelphia. May God reward him for his faithful service.

In like manner, our participation in the life of Christ requires the team outfit. And here the Lord has mandated that the Church confer such an outfit. Christ's team members are brought up to the supernatural majors through baptism. It is this divinely ordained sacrament that puts a Major League uniform on the soul of the Christian who is expected to play at the highest level — to live a life of exemplary virtue — to hear and act on the universal call to holiness.

Baptism grafts us onto the very Body of Christ. Stop and ponder a moment that the very same Holy Spirit with his grace that filled the divine nature of Christ is imparted to us! Remember that baptism leaves an indelible mark on the soul, forever identifying the Christian as a spiritual Major Leaguer. Now it is up to the Catholic Christian to strive for their Hall of Fame: heaven. Always aided by God's grace, of course, for Jesus tells us emphatically: "I am the vine, you are the branches. He who abides in me, and I in him, he it is that bears much fruit, for apart from me you can do nothing" (Jn 15:5).

One final point on the uniform: It must be earned every

45

game and every season. Perform poorly and a trip to the minors is waiting, at best, or a career ended, at worst. Pitchers must earn victories, batters produce hits and runs, fielders play stellar defense, and all make decisions on the field that exhibit good judgment. A player who does not employ his skills for the good of the team is exiled one way or another.

It is so, too, with our life in Christ. We must keep our uniform clean and in good condition. We must wear it always and not just don it when convenient.

Recall the parable our blessed Lord recounted in which the guest at a wedding feast attended without the proper garment. He was ordered bound and thrown out of the feast to where there was wailing and gnashing of teeth. The point that Jesus was making is that we must enter the ball field (Kingdom) with the uniform given to us in baptism, having persevered in faith to the end with a career full of love and good works.

Our supernatural garment is fashioned over a career of prayer, fasting, and almsgiving. This is the spiritual Triple Crown. Prayer is the batting average, fasting qualifies as a home run, and almsgiving produces RBIs. Our Lord's teammates run the base paths of holiness through lively faith, unwavering hope, and burning charity. A Christian who fails to live the Gospel injunction to love is not worthy of the uniform. Baptismal grace may be squandered through indifference or mediocrity. Let's resolve to expend the effort to live up to our divine calling.

To close this meditation, let's ponder the position on the team. Let's start by contemplating that every atom in the universe was created by God the Father and he sustains all creation by his loving providence. Recall what Jesus tells us: "Even the hairs of your head are all numbered" (Lk 12:7). So, we conclude, nothing is left to chance and there are no coincidences. We really need to see everything that happens as coming from the hand of God.

Apply this in the natural order to our great game of baseball. We can conclude that God's hand is in every detail. For example, early on baseball settled on nine positions. The best reason I can give for this is that Our Lord had ordained nine positions in heaven before the creation of man. Here I'm talking about angels, and not the California variety. God established the nine choirs and they fit the scorebook nomenclature perfectly.

#	Position	Orders
1	Pitcher	Seraphim
2	Catcher	Cherubim
3	First Base	Thrones
4	Second Base	Dominions
5	Third Base	Virtues
6	Shortstop	Powers
7	Left Field	Principalities
8	Center Field	Angels
9	Right Field	Archangels

As a manager sets the lineup and directs the assignments of each player, so, too, God the Father established his lineup in the supernatural order (and the natural order as well) and directs the action of his team from above. Each angel has a specific position and assignment in the heavenly contest.

Corresponding to the position that scores putouts, the seraphim are known as burning angels, or angels of fire. Thus they are the pitchers in the game hurling praises like Promethean heaters (fastballs) as they worship around the throne of God. The cherubim, who are portrayed as youthful and plump, are at No. 2 corresponding to the catcher. Note that the archangels are No. 9 in the order corresponding to right field. Just as right fielders have strong arms so, too, the archangels. They often come out of nowhere with laser like throws. Consider Michael throwing out Lucifer when he rebelled and became Satan; or Raphael pinch hitting for Tobit in finding a wife; or Gabriel, emerging from the portals of heaven for the Annunciation, the opportunity to provide an assist in the drama of the Incarnation.

Just as it is in heaven, baseball replicates this harmony and structure in positioning the players for defense. Each position with the same goal: to score outs and prevent runs. But each with different skills, abilities, duties, and placement. One field and nine positions mirror the supernatural nature of the Church with many members but one body. Saint Paul put this succinctly when he wrote: "For just as the body is one and has many members, and all the members of the body, though many, are one body, so it is with Christ. For by one Spirit we were all baptized into one body — Jews or Greeks, slaves or free — and all were made to drink of one Spirit" (1 Cor 12:12–13).

Paul then goes on to explain the positions:

> Now you are the body of Christ and individually members of it. And God has appointed in the church first apostles, second prophets, third teachers, then workers of miracles, then healers, helpers, administrators, speakers in various kinds of tongues. Are all apostles? Are all prophets? Are all teachers? Do all work miracles? Do all possess gifts of healing? Do all speak in tongues? Do all interpret? But earnestly desire the higher gifts. (1 Corinthians 12:27–31).

The spiritually astute baseball fan immediately recognizes that Our Lord assigns the positions and, like the baseball team manager, will do everything possible to put us in a position to excel and to win. We must realize the great dignity conferred on us by baptism by our Father in heaven. How we were not just made a member of a ball club but a member of the Catholic Church incorporated into the Body of Christ. That in Christ we have the fulfillment of God's plan for our life who "chose us in him before the foundation of the world" (Eph 1:4).

Teammates, God made us for himself. Our singular purpose in life is to know, love, and serve God. We do this especially by playing our position in the supernatural ballpark. The position that God gives us is our vocation. A vocation is God's personal call to holiness and the path we must take to sanctity. God calls some to the religious vocation, most to marriage, and others to single life. In these states of life is where we find our heavenly mission. Then God gives us talents to employ for his glory in this state in life: teachers, healers, builders, singers, painters, designers, writers, managers, financiers, and so many others. It is the use of these talents, for which we can't take credit, that God will ask for an account. How well we use our abilities and time to play our position will determine how many victories over sin and selfishness. It will determine how many teammates we helped advance along the path of holiness by our example and words. And most importantly, it will determine how many runs we drove in; how many of our brothers and sisters we brought to the Faith and to Christ.

Finally, let us recall that in the Gospel Jesus tells his apostles: "You did not choose me, but I chose and appointed you that you should go and bear fruit and that your fruit should abide; so that whatever you ask the Father in my name, he may give it to you" (Jn 15:16). While Father Allan may have pursued his baseball aspirations, saving baseball games is not to be compared with saving souls. He played the position Our Lord chose for him by answering the call to the priesthood.

As the Lord says to Jeremiah: "Before I formed you in the womb I knew you, / and before you were born, I consecrated you; / I appointed you a prophet to the nations" (Jer 1:5). He says that also to each and every one of us. Have recourse to him through his Catholic Church where you received the immense gift of the Major League uniform in baptism. God will show you your path to holiness. Parents, teach your children to pray to Jesus that he will direct them to his chosen path for them in life. With the help of their guardian angels, they will find the vocation for which they were destined.

One parting point: The Catholic Church teaches that the Father has assigned each of his children a guardian angel. Our guardian angels guide us, inspire us, and, most important of all, protect us against sin and error. Like first and third base coaches, our guardian angel helps us advance along the base paths of holiness. Pray to your guardian angel for help for yourself and those whom you love.

——

QUESTIONS FOR REFLECTION - THE INTENTIONAL WALK

⚾ BALL ONE

Can I give examples of how Divine Providence has guided my life? Do I see every tiny circumstance as coming from his loving plan for me? Do I thank God for his loving protection, help, and guidance?

⚾ BALL TWO

Baptism confers on me the dignity of a child of God — that is, the spiritual Major League uniform. Do I cultivate an appreciation and a deeper understanding of my calling through reading Scripture? What are the concrete ways I am practicing to become more like Christ?

⚾ BALL THREE

Do I find time to study my faith or do I just leave it up to the homily to feed me. Do I realize God has a specific position he wants me to play and that I can only drive in those runners to heaven whom God puts on base in my life? Whom have I talked to about Christ this past week? Month? Year?

⚾ BALL FOUR

The three theological virtues are faith, hope, and charity, representing first, second, and third base on the diamond, without which we can't make it home. Can I explain why these virtues are theological and how they unite me to my most loving God, the Holy Trinity?

—ON DECK—

St. Frances de Sales (*HOF*)

"When God created the world, he commanded each tree to bear fruit after its kind and even so — he bids Christians — the living trees of his Church — to bring forth fruits of devotion, each one according to his kind and vocation. A different exercise of devotion is required of each — the noble, the artisan, the servant, the prince, the maiden, and the wife; and furthermore such practice must be modified according to the strength, the calling, and the duties of each individual."

4TH INNING

Pitching:
Our Lord's Perfect Pitch

You, therefore, must be perfect, as your heavenly Father is perfect.
— Matthew 5:48

The pitcher's mound — the sanctuary and heart of the diamond — is the elevated ground that is unique to this mysterious sport.

One who loves baseball and the Catholic Faith sees it as not just the focal point of all the games activity but a reflection of the elevated ground in the Bible: Mount Sinai in the Old Testament where God appeared to Moses in the burning bush, who later hurled the Ten Commandments; and the Sermon on the Mount in the New Testament where our divine Savior threw his perfect game.

Consider that the noble art of pitching mirrors the Catholic Faith in that perfection is actually possible, even if extremely elusive. This is because pitching, like hitting, involves both success and failure. Take, for example, Hall of Fame pitchers with over 300 victories — pitchers like Warren Spahn, Nolan Ryan, Greg Maddux, and Roger Clemens. Spahn lost 245 games, Ryan 292, and Maddux 227, while Clemens lost only 184. Each of them lost more games than teams play in an entire season. Among these all-time greats there is one accomplishment none of them achieved: a perfect game!

Achieving perfection is one of the rarest accomplishments in sport, and baseball is among the few in which its possible. Just how rare is it? The Baseball Almanac reports that over the 150 years of Major League Baseball history, and more than 218,400 games played, there have been twenty-three official perfect games by the current definition. No pitcher has ever thrown more than one. In fact, there are eighty-three pitchers in the Hall of Fame at this writing and only seven of those — Cy Young, Addie Joss, Jim Bunning, Sandy Koufax, Catfish Hunter, Randy Johnson, and Roy Halladay — pitched a perfect contest. There has not been one pitched since 2012, when three were recorded.

A perfect game is achieved when the pitcher retires twenty-seven straight batters over the course of nine innings: no runs, hits, or errors. To qualify as a perfect game a pitcher must retire every batter that comes to the plate, even if the game extends into extra innings.

Two players have pitched perfect games into extra innings — Harvey Haddix and Pedro Martinez — only to lose in extra frames. In fact, Haddix pitched what many baseball experts consider the "greatest game ever pitched." On May 26, 1959, Haddix threw twelve perfect innings against the Milwaukee Braves before losing the game in the thirteenth inning when he gave up a three-run homer. In a strange twist, the celebrating Braves messed up running the bases on the winning blast. After review, the score was changed from 3–0 to 2–0. Next day, the score was changed again to 1–0 when the home run was changed to a double due to the Braves' base-running fiasco. Nevertheless, Haddix lost his perfect game and the game itself.

While playing for Montreal, Martinez took a perfect game into the tenth inning, but lost his perfect game when the twenty-eight batter doubled. Martinez did garner the win in that one.

A pitcher cannot achieve perfection on his own, of course. If a runner reaches base on an error, it will ruin a pitcher's perfect game. Even fan interference can theoretically spoil a perfect game. Not only that, but the umpires must also get all their calls right. Ask Armando Galarraga, who pitched for Detroit in 2010 and lost his bid for perfection with two outs in the ninth on a blown call at first. Moreover, the team must score to support the pitcher. Perfection is rare and it takes a total team and organizational effort.

While a pitcher may take the mound determined to get every

batter out, the odds are astronomically high against his success. After that first hit or runner reaches base, the pitcher must once again strive to get every hitter out — to commit himself anew to perfection in an ineluctably imperfect situation. Only the future can be perfect. You can't run out the clock in baseball. You must get the outs.

The pitcher remains at the heart of the action. He has the ball even though his team is on defense (baseball, like the Gospel, is full of paradoxes). Moreover, though the team wins or loses the game through collective effort, only the pitcher of record (like the prophets in the Bible), gets credit by name for the win or the loss. He alone must face every opposing hitter, as he attempts to assert his supremacy over the hitter. One pitch sets up another. One out dictates the next out. Behind the pitcher and home plate are his teammates, eight players moving and adjusting to the situation as the count changes — as does the number of outs, the number of opposing players occupying bases, and the tendency of the batter to pull the ball, hit straight away, or hit to all fields, with varying degrees of power. Whatever the game's circumstances, the pitcher needs the outs!

Pitching, like many things in life and in the Church, seems simple. Throw strikes, change speeds, and work quickly — the latter proves an advantage to fielders poised in ready position in case the ball is hit their way. Three things are integral to successful pitching: velocity, movement, and location. In the majors, the consensus is that location is most important. Take your pick on velocity and movement after that. One thing is certain, you cannot get Major League hitters out with velocity alone. A pitcher must throw strikes and then those strikes must be where the batter can't hit them. Control is tantamount to success. Lack of control is a career-ending condition.

Nowhere is the need for control more evident than in the perfect game. The pitcher retiring the side inning after inning is almost always in command of his pitches. He is not working into deep three-ball counts, because a walk spoils perfection. There can be no batters hit by the pitch or even a passed ball on a third strike. To ensure no hits, the number of "mistake" pitches over the fat part of plate or in the hitter's wheelhouse must be avoided or kept to the very minimum. And the pitcher must control his emotions. In summary, ball control, self-control, and mental control — no wildness.

Now many pitchers have struggled with wildness, and most minor league hurlers don't make the Big Show because they can't master locating their pitches and throwing what are called quality strikes. In fact, many of the elite hurlers struggled with wildness early in their careers — Mickey Lolich, Sandy Koufax, and Nolan Ryan, among many others, had to work hard to gain control. In fact, lack of control even overcomes talent.

Here the story of Steve Dalkowski comes to mind. In baseball annals, he may have been the fastest pitcher ever to fire the ball. His is a story of a gifted arm without any semblance of control. It is related in *The Baseball Almanac* as follows:

> The fastest pitcher ever may have been 1950s phenom and flameout Steve Dalkowski. Dalkowski signed with the Orioles in 1957 at age 21. After nine years of erratic pitching, he was released in 1966, never having made it to the Major Leagues. Despite his failure, he has been described as the fastest pitcher ever.
>
> Ted Williams once stood in a spring training batting cage and took one pitch from Dalkowski. Williams swore he never saw the ball and claimed that Dalkowski probably was the fastest pitcher who ever lived. Others who claimed he was the fastest ever were Paul Richards, Harry Brecheen and Earl Weaver. They all thought he was faster than Bob Feller and Walter Johnson, though none of them probably saw Johnson pitch.
>
> It was estimated that Dalkowski's fastball at times reached 105 mph. Dalkowski was not physically imposing, standing only 5'8" and wearing thick glasses. He had legendary

wildness, which kept him out of the Major Leagues. In 995 minor league innings, he walked 1,354 batters and struck out 1,396. He walked 21 in one minor league game and struck out 21 in another. In high school he pitched a no-hitter while walking 18 and striking out 18.

He threw 283 pitches in a complete game against Aberdeen and once threw 120 pitches in only two innings. He played in nine leagues in nine years.

In 1963, for Elmira he finally started throwing strikes. During spring training in 1964, Dalkowski was with the Major League club. After fielding a sacrifice bunt by pitcher Jim Bouton in spring training, Dalkowski's arm went dead and he never recovered. He drifted to various jobs and landed in Bakersfield, California, where he was arrested many times for fighting.

He once threw a ball at least 450 feet on a bet. He was supposed to throw the ball from the outfield wall to home plate, but he threw it well above the plate into the press box. He once threw a pitch so hard that the catcher missed the ball and it shattered an umpire's mask. Dalkowski was the basis for wild fastball pitcher Nuke LaLoosh in the movie *Bull Durham*.

The Steve Dalkowski story is all too familiar. A player with extraordinary potential does not succeed in making it to the Major Leagues. So many factors come together to affect a person's once-in-a-lifetime opportunity. Maybe Dalkowski's career-ending injury would not have occurred with better coaching, or if he had been with a different team, at a different time.

The Dalkowski story proves that baseball is a complex sport and throwing hard is no substitute for pitching. Success depends on knowledge, control, poise, experience, discipline, preparation, and character. It requires the player to be mature and learn from those who say, "I wish I knew what I know now back when I could still do it."

The mystery of human freedom and free will is often on full display in the heat of competition, especially prolonged daily competition, as is the case on the diamond. The lesson is clear: Success requires effort with the full support of the team and the organization. Talent alone does not always translate into success. The foundation for success is CONTROL!

There are two Catholic mysteries to explore that are hidden in the art of pitching. The first is that perfection is possible; our blessed Lord told us so. A second mystery is the absolute indispensability of belonging to the Church with its supernatural support guiding us to a career exceeding 300 wins. The demands placed upon the professional pitcher are daunting. No less challenging are the demands of the Gospel on the committed Catholic. It takes supernatural strength to have Major League control in the spiritual realm. Our Lord told his apostles this directly at the Last Supper: "I am the vine, you are the branches. He who abides in me, and I in him, he it is that will bear much fruit, for apart from me you can do nothing" (Jn 15:5).

Let's first explore the mystery of perfection. Our Lord took to the hill in a park overlooking the Sea of Galilee. He was near Capernaum, where he multiplied the loaves and fishes and fed the five thousand. Here on this elevated ground Our Lord pitched the perfect game.

Turning the world's conceptions and ideas on their heads, he offered up the dramatic teaching of the Eight Beatitudes:

Blessed are the poor in spirit, for theirs is the kingdom of heaven.
Blessed are they who mourn for they shall be comforted.
Blessed are the meek, for they shall inherit the earth.
Blessed are those who hunger and thirst for righteousness, for they shall be satisfied.
Blessed are the merciful, for they shall obtain mercy.
Blessed are the pure in of heart, for they shall see God.
Blessed are the peacemakers, for they shall be called sons

of God.

Blessed are those who are persecuted for righteousness' sake, for theirs is the kingdom of heaven. (Matthew 5:3–10)

Then Our Lord, in the same sermon, offered up a radically new perspective on anger, adultery, divorce, taking oaths, retaliation, and love of enemies. This is followed with the beautiful exhortations on prayer, fasting, and almsgiving — there is the spiritual triple crown again. Within this sermon, our divine Savior then offered the perfect pitch: "You, therefore, must be perfect, as your heavenly Father is perfect" (Mt 5:48).

Jesus is not laying a harsh burden on weak human shoulders. Just as the manager does not expect a perfect game from his pitcher, Our Lord does not have unrealistic expectations. Like any good coach, Jesus is articulating a vision of what the ideal team member should be like — that is, what is required to play Major League ball in his Kingdom. The same quality required of a star pitcher is necessary for success in the spiritual life — CONTROL.

Just as wildness is a sure ticket out of the Major Leagues, wildness is a recipe for exclusion from heaven's team. Saint Paul pulls no punches when, like a good coach, he exhorts us to be Major Leaguers. He writes, "Now the works of the flesh are plain: immorality, impurity, licentiousness, idolatry, sorcery, enmity, strife, jealously, anger, selfishness, dissension, party spirit, envy, drunkenness, carousing and the like. I warn you … that those who do such things shall not inherit the kingdom of God" (Gal 5:19–21). We cannot be wild in our thoughts, actions, temper, diet, speech, or dress. This wildness is a sure path off Our Lord's team if not corrected.

But Paul immediately after gives us the formula for Major League virtue and control with pitches for strikes. He tells us: "but the fruit of the Spirit is love, joy, peace, patience, kindness, goodness faithfulness, gentleness, self-control; against such there is no law. And those who belong to Christ Jesus have crucified the flesh with its passions" (Gal 5:22-24). Yes indeed, the Catholic gift in the

Sacrament of Confirmation plants in us the fruits of the Holy Spirit!

While on the topic of control, realize that the beauty of Jesus' teaching is that there is no misunderstanding of the nature of sin and the weakness of the flesh. At the same time, Jesus, through his Church, proclaims and provides access to remedies for sin and evil. Our Divine Savior sends us to the mound to contend with the forces of darkness that are always seeking our downfall.

Meditate on your daily challenge: Sin and occasions to fall lurk all around us every day. Jesus knows we may get shelled in the first inning, pitch ourselves into several jams, lose a few games, and make some rookie mistakes. But just as players grow in competency and hone their skills, God gives us the gift of time precisely to grow toward that ideal of perfection. What else could be the purpose of life than to form ourselves in the image of Christ so that we are worthy to enter eternal life in heaven — the truly Big Show.

Now just as the perfect game, and for that matter a stellar winning record, requires the support of the entire organization — player personnel on the field, capable defense, potent offense, attentive coaching, a solid game plan, knowledge of the opposition, and even competent adjudication of the rules — so, too, holiness and advancing in perfection requires the collective effort of the Church. Just as a player needs to subordinate himself to the demands of the team, so the Catholic must consider himself a member with one role among many in the mystical Body of Christ. Major League Baseball is strictly a flawed human institution. The Church on the other hand is both a human and divine institution. It is God the Father's plan that his children accept the authority handed down by Christ to his apostles and love the Church as they love Christ himself. For we find the remedies to our weakness in Christ's body, the Church.

How does one pitch the perfect game? How does one advance in spiritual perfection? It is a step-by-step process of working through the innings of life and surrounding ourselves with teammates and coaches who can help us on our way. In fact, it is a great blessing to find a good priest to be a regular confessor and to seek out a spiritual director. We always need to work on the weak points of our game, and a coach in the Kingdom can be so important. The saints availed themselves of these coaches and often the confessors were their spiritual directors.

Holiness requires, first and foremost, the elimination of mortal sin from our lives. This is sin which is objectively grave and undertaken in the full knowledge of the action's evil, with our full consent. After we have conquered serious sin on a consistent basis (which is not saying we may not fall back into serious sin—that's always a possibility), we then try to weed out less serious, or venial, sins. Finally, Christian perfection demands the elimination of the small ways we offend God through lack of charity or neglect of good works.

This is essentially what it takes to conform completely to the will of God. It is all for love of the game! Just as a pitcher does not serve up a perfect game alone, so a soul cannot attain perfection alone. God offers the support of the Church first and foremost through the sacraments. Each sacrament is a channel of grace. This is the means by which God pours the divine life of the Holy Spirit into the soul.

We cannot overestimate the power and efficacy of the sacraments. They are the seven conditions for living a holy life and correspond to the seven conditions needed for a winning team. Let's review.

Baptism removes original sin and confers on the soul membership in the Church. The baseball counterpart is wearing of the uniform. Penance is the healing sacrament available after we fall from grace, the wild pitches and bean balls we throw. Baseball has its injured reserve list as a time-out for healing. Confirmation advances us to spiritual maturity and strengthens the soul to suffer for Christ. Here we learn control. Baseball appoints each player a position on the team and its provides an understanding of how to play it well.

The Eucharist is the Bread of Life, the central mystery of the Faith, without which all other efforts are futile. Here the baseball itself is the life-giving connection to the game. Anointing of the sick is a gift for healing and spiritual strength at the time of death. The baseball counterpart is treatment and training to restore physical health. Marriage gives the Church mothers and fathers. Baseball has no players without Mom. The last sacrament is holy orders, which ordains priests and affords the Church bishops and the papacy for governance. Baseball correspondingly has coaches, managers, front-office personnel, and its commissioner for governance. Without access to the sacraments, it is very difficult to pitch on Our Lord's team. One cannot give what one does not have. We should avail ourselves of the sacraments and make them the center of our life. After all, the Church is more of a hospital for sinners than a society for saints, as many saints and popes have explained.

Finally, the Lord gives us the example of superb control and perfection when during his thirty-three-year career on earth he piled up more wins than Cy Young (Major League career record 511 wins). What is Our Lord's example? It is simply this: He prayed. All four Gospels reveal the depth of our Savior's prayer life: before beginning his ministry he prays forty days in the desert; then, before he chooses the twelve, he prays all night; after curing Peter's mother-in-law, he rises early to pray; Jesus prayed alone before he asked the apostles, "Who do the people say that I am"; he went up the mountain to pray before the Transfiguration; Jesus was praying in a certain place when the disciples asked him, "Lord, teach us to pray"; he prayed at Lazarus's tomb; he prayed at the Last Supper. And Jesus prayed in the garden the night before he died, asking Peter, James, and John to pray with him one hour.

We should ask ourselves how well we follow the Lord's example. For the true measure of our love for God is found in our prayer life. Give Our Lord an hour a week before the tabernacle, say the Rosary daily, and spend fifteen minutes in meditation on the Gospels. A Major League career requires Major League effort. Pray always, as Saint Paul exhorts.

It is a tragedy of immense magnitude for the Catholic

to gloss over Our Lord's words in the Sermon on the Mount. "Be perfect as your heavenly Father is perfect" is not just a sentimental or rhetorical flourish. Our Lord sends all his players to the mound, just like the prophets of old, to face the enemy of the people of God. Every day the Catholic contends with a competing evil nine, racking up a record of wins and losses, strike outs and an earned Run average — the triple crown of pitching. And like the pitchers of record in a game, the credit for a win or loss is given by name. We will see this in the book of judgment mentioned so often in Revelation. To be a serious Catholic requires wisdom, understanding, counsel, fortitude, knowledge, piety, and fear of the Lord. These are the seven gifts of the Holy Spirit available to the entire pitching staff and given to us in confirmation. Know your faith, love your Church, serve your God — before it's too late to take the mound and your opportunity to pitch a perfect game is gone.

— —

QUESTIONS FOR REFLECTION - THE INTENTIONAL WALK

BALL ONE

What is my attitude toward the Church? Do I see it as divine because Jesus founded it with his blood and it is the means by which he gives himself to us? Or do I discredit the Church because it is human and so many members have given scandal?

BALL TWO

Do I pursue the triple crown through prayer, fasting, and almsgiving? Do I realize that my measure of love for Our Lord is the depth of my prayer life, which entails talking to the one I love?

BALL THREE

As a pitcher needs control to excel in the big leagues, do I use the gifts of the sacraments, especially confession once a month and frequent holy Communion, to strengthen my self-control, knowing that apart from Christ I can do nothing?

BALL FOUR

Do I fast on Fridays or abstain from meat realizing that the need for penance strenghtens me? Do I give alms sacrificially, recognizing the biblical practice of giving the first 10% to God who has accomplished all we have done?

—ON DECK—

St. Augustine of Hippo (*HOF*)

"Fasting cleanses the soul, raises the mind, subjects one's flesh to the spirit, renders the heart contrite and humble, scatters the clouds of concupiscence, quenches the fires of lust, kindles the true light of chastity."

5ᵀᴴ INNING

Hitting:
The Bat, the Tree, and the Cross

If any man would come after me, let him deny himself and take up his cross and follow me. — Matthew 16:24

The great drama of baseball plays out at home plate. The hitter takes up the bat and enters his sanctuary, the batter's box, and seeks to assert supremacy over home plate. He faces, metaphorically, the powers of darkness in the pitcher, who, too, is looking to establish dominance over the plate. Opposing forces clash with the pitcher hurling Promethean heat against the hitter's violent parry with his bat. One will succeed and one will not. The whole furious engagement of hitters with pitchers continues until a victor emerges. While the ball is the namesake and essence of the game, the wooden bat alone possesses the game's central mystique. In the baseball, as in salvation history, wood is the instrument of defeat and the instrument of victory.

Ted Williams could relate to both these dimensions of hitting. "Baseball is the only field of endeavor where a man can succeed three times out of ten and be considered a good performer," said the hitting great. The Splendid Splinter, whose one desire in life was to be known as the greatest hitter who ever lived, understood profoundly that like life hitting is more failure than success. Yet, despite the failure rate, you can imagine that when Williams was on deck, the pitcher was already muttering to himself — damn, he's up next! Williams' bat was the object of fear for many a pitcher.

Williams arguably is one of the greatest hitters the world

has ever seen. On September 28, 1941, the last day of that season, he played in a doubleheader against the Philadelphia Athletics. Ted lashed out six hits in eight at bats to boost his batting average to .406. Williams was the first player to reach that coveted batting average since Bill Terry hit .400 in 1930. Williams is also the last man to hit .400 in a season.

Here is a bit of hitting trivia: another Red Sox great, Wade Boggs, never batted .400 in a season but managed to hit .401 over a 162-game span from June 9, 1985, to June 6, 1986. Moreover, Boggs owns the highest batting average in Fenway Park history at .369. That is eight points higher than second-place Ted Williams. Put the bat in the hands of these supremely talented ball players and the result was often a hit or a run or both — more than three times out of ten! However, as Williams' laconic quote reminds the baseball faithful, the game is one of failure. Fans also realize — as many in other sports would acknowledge — that hitting Major League pitching is the most difficult endeavor in the sport.

George Brett is the last player to flirt with the .400-mark. In 1980, he achieved a batting average for the season of .390. There may never be another .400 hitter — not because today's hitters are less talented. Pitchers have become ever more devilish — and fresh, as managers often use relief pitchers earlier in the game and more frequently. They are also using science to their advantage these days. Let's explore both of the aspects that have impacted batting averages over the last half-century.

Like the serpent in the garden tempting our first parents, in order to take the tree of the knowledge of good and evil "out of play," Major League pitchers have from the beginning conspired to confound, confuse, and overpower the hitter.

First, pitching has evolved to an unparalleled level of specialization. Consider, for example, that Levi Meyerle hit an astounding .492 for the Philadelphia Athletics in 1871, in what was then the National Association. That was before the mound was moved back to sixty feet six inches and before any modern-day sophistication in pitching motion (pitchers were required to "pitch" underhand to the batter). Pitchers often got shelled in those early years. But like the serpent in the garden, pitchers learned how to use cunning against hitters.

In the earliest days, pitchers would throw dozens of pitches to a single batter hoping to frustrate him enough to swing at a bad offering. Balls were called on every third "unfair" pitch and it took nine balls before the batter walked, instead of the modern era's four. When Meyerle was playing, pitchers not only had to pitch underhand with no running start, but they had to limit their throwing motions from nine o'clock to three o'clock. Wily hurlers started stretching the throwing-motion rules restrictions, learning to submarine or sidearm the pitch with increasing speed.

Rules restricting the pitcher's motion were completely removed in 1884. Batting averages naturally dropped, as well as run production.

Then came the lengthening of the distance from home plate to the pitching rubber. In the 1880s the distance moved from fifty feet to fifty-five feet five inches to the current sixty feet six inches. As a result, batting averages began to climb again through the "dead ball era" into the "live ball era."

When Ted Williams hit over .400 in 1941 (the year Joe DiMaggio recorded his 56-game hitting streak) things were about to change again for the hitters. Another element of difficulty was being introduced. This time it was the relief pitcher. Joe Page of the Yankees is considered the first modern closer, appearing in 278 games from 1946 to 1950. In the 1950s Jim Konstanty, Elroy Face, Lindy McDaniel, and Hoyt Wilhelm made relief pitching a staple of the roster. Bullpen aces were on every roster in the 1960s, and in the decade that followed these specialists were winning MVP awards.

Today, every team has or needs a closer, a set-up man, and mid-reliever. Pitching staffs are built from the closer back to the starters, with the perceptive fan understanding what all managers know: The last six outs of a game are often the most difficult to get. The result is that hitters are not getting third and fourth looks at the same pitcher. They often face a right-hander followed by a left-hander and back to a right-hander. When the starting pitcher's velocity drops, a live arm is on the way to the mound from the bullpen.

The Major League hurler not only fires the ball to the plate in fractions of a second, but he changes the speed of his pitches deceptively. He may also use a variety of motions and deliveries to keep a batter off-balance. (Fernando Valenzuela was famous for rolling his eyes up to the sky.)

A good pitcher also exploits a hitter's weakness. Is he a sucker for a high fastball? Does he have trouble laying off pitches that are down and in?

The hitter tries his best to guess which pitch is coming, watching for the angle of release and the spin of the ball as cues. Still, even the best hitters frequently look hapless and ineffective, swinging at pitches out of the strike zone or merely waving at one that fooled them. Success proves fleeting from game to game. A batter can have four hits one outing and strike out four times the next. Within the same game a towering home run can be followed by a bases-loaded strike out. The failure rate statistics are stark and unrelenting.

Then there is the science of it all. A 95-mile-per-hour fastball that leaves the pitchers hand 53 to 55 feet from the plate is traveling 139.33 feet per second. The pitch will reach the batter in .434 seconds. A change-up sailing along at 80 miles per hour travels 117 feet per second and will arrive in .469 seconds. The .035 seconds may not seem like much, but when a hitter has only .2 seconds to swing and hit the pitch, that difference is crucial to success or failure. The ball can be reached by the bat in only 2 feet of the pitch's path, leaving a window of about fifteen-thousandths of a second to make contact. Moreover, many pitchers in the big leagues reach velocities in the high 90s, reducing fractions of a second to even leaner fractions of a second. Couple this with off-speed stuff floating deceptively in the high 70s and it's no mystery why batters face futility seven times or more out of ten. Major League hitting is, well, nearly impossible for mere mortals. All this conspires against a hitter ever batting .400 over the course of a season again.

Now, if the name of the game (and its very essence) is derived from the ball, the focus, fury, and violence of the competitive clash of Major League competition comes from the end of the bat. It is true that nothing happens without the ball; it must be put in play. But, as noted earlier, the bat stands out as central to baseball's mystique; it's the instrument of victory. Those who score more runs are victorious. And it is the bat as the instrument of victory that produces the most exciting moments and vivid memories. Some of these victories come at a moment when all seems lost. Let's recall some stories from baseball lore that come to us from the end of the bat.

First, there is Babe Ruth's called shot at Wrigley Field during the 1934 World Series against the Cubs. Knowledgeable fans ponder this when attending a game in those venerable confines, even to this day. Bill Mazeroski's dramatic seventh-game, ninth-inning home run at Forbes Field to win the 1960 World Series also comes to mind. Almost equally evocative was Joe Carter's blast off Mitch Williams in game six of the 1993 World Series, giving the Blue Jays the victory over the surging Phillies. Another victorious blast was the "shot heard around the world," Bobby Thomson's home run at the Polo Grounds that gave the New York Giants the National League Pennant over the Dodgers. Who can forget the iconic moment in Fenway Park in 1975 when Carlton Fisk's long fly ball to left stayed fair for a home run and kept the Red Sox' hopes alive against the Big Red Machine? (They lost the Series in game seven, of course.)

The drama off the end of the bat is not always a home run. In the classic World Series struggle between the Yankees and Diamondbacks in 2001, Luis Gonzalez tapped a soft bloop single over Derek Jeter in the ninth inning to win the game and the series. The Yankee Hall of Fame reliever, Mariano Rivera, thus suffered his only loss in his many postseason playoff appearances.

The game's ending was providential. Although he lost, Mariano gave thanks to God, because if the Yankees had won, the victory parade in New York would have delayed teammate's Enrique Wilson's flight home to the Dominican Republic. Enrique Wilson would have been on American Airlines flight 587, which crashed in Queens shortly after takeoff. Enrique had been booked on that flight. There were no survivors.

Finally, the bat is the instrument of victory in those "pulled from the brink of extinction moments." In 1986, the California Angels were one strike away from their first trip to the World Series when Donnie Moore surrendered a home run to Dave Henderson and the Red Sox went on to win game five in extra innings. The Sox then returned to Boston and beat the Angels in games six and seven to make it to the World Series against the Mets.

Then, in game six of that series, it was Boston's turn to collapse. This time it would be a simple ground ball off the bat of Mookie Wilson that would score the winning run. Two Red Sox relievers had been within one strike of winning the series, but Wilson's ground ball went through first baseman Bill Buckner's legs. Boston lost the deciding game and the Curse of the Bambino (the Red Sox inability to win a championship after trading Babe Ruth) continued.

A few points about the Major League bats that provide these glorious moments for the victors: The professional leagues, where the contest is played at the highest level of the game's virtues, continue to use bats fashioned from wood. Unpaid players in schools, colleges, and elsewhere have gone to metal. In the professional ranks, however, the use of wood is infallible doctrine, and to change to another substance would irreparably alter the mystique of the sport. Why is this so? Because metal bats do not break. This may seem like an advantage, but to the pitcher standing a mere fifty feet away from a Major League hitter after delivering a pitch, a metal bat smashing a ball back through the mound could quickly end many a career.

Metal bats would also limit the pitcher's ability to throw inside. Mariano Rivera possessed a God-given (his words) cut fastball that sailed to the inside on left-handed batters. He was notorious for breaking bats — one is even on display in the Hall of Fame. Imagine pitching inside with bats that don't break. What would be soft outs and weakly hit balls could be muscled by pros into the outfield for hits. The change would forever alter the game.

Finally, check how bats are made on YouTube. The species of wood is critical. The majority of the bats are made of either sugar maple or white ash. However, the favored wood in the last 15-20 years has shifted to rock maple. The rock maple is harder and hits the ball further, making it a hit with Major League players looking to hit more home runs. The downside is a smaller sweet spot on the barrel of the bat. Ash is a much more forgiving wood, with a larger sweet spot, allowing more control of where you would want to hit the ball.

No matter the species, each bat is milled to a specific size and weight as specified by the player. Not only that, the player can adjust the bat's length and the thickness of the handle and barrel to his liking. After each bat is carefully finished, the manufacturer stamps the player's name on it before sending it on to the team and into the battle.

Those of us who played baseball probably recall using a particular model in the '50s, '60s, or '70s when there were no aluminum bats. The Jackie Robinson model had a thick handle and barrel and was heavy. Johnny Bench and Al Kaline models had slim handles and wide barrels, while Mickey Mantle's was thicker toward the knob and a bit heavier than other models. The point is, they were and still are personalized. Bryce Harper and Manny Machado models are popular today.

Finally, players sometimes exhibit strange sentiments when it comes to their bats. Shoeless Joe Jackson insisted on having his bats hibernate in the South Carolina winter to stay warm. Richie Ashburn, the great Phillies player and announcer, once remarked that he slept with his bats. Orlando Cepeda, a Giants power hitter, would throw away a bat after a single hit, believing there were only so many hits in a stick and you could not be sure any were remaining. Ted Williams would send bats back to Louisville, allegedly because of mistakes made by the lathe operator of a few thousandths of an inch. And R. A. Dickey of knuckleball fame named his bats.

Moving from the diamond to the divine, the spiritual-minded fan immediately sees the biblical connections to two profound events in salvation history: the fall of the human race from grace by the sin and defeat of our first parents; and the glorious victory won by Christ on the wood of the cross on Calvary. Thus we see the wood as the instrument of defeat in the Old Testament and instrument of victory in the New Testament. And this has enormous implications for each and every Catholic's performance on the field of life. For just as without the bat there is no victory on the baseball field, without the cross there is no victory over sin and death. And just as the pitcher uses every device and opportunity to neutralize the hitter, so does the devil seek to tempt Christ's teammates away from the cross' significance in their own lives. Let's deal with the devil first.

The Fall of Man is recounted in the beginning (Big Inning) of the Book of Genesis. The devil approaches Eve in the ballpark of paradise and fires an array of pitches at her to disturb her relationship with God. Here, the wood of the tree is of central importance. Satan minimizes its importance with cunning and curve balls. The fruit was desirable, so he told Eve she should eat it; that she would not die; that she would become like a god; that she would have knowledge of good and evil apart from God, which God, in his supposed selfishness, was willfully denying her so as to keep Eve subservient. Eve partakes of the fruit and urges Adam to do likewise.

Strike one, strike two, and strike three, and God called them out. Our first parents committed the original sin with their disobedience. Thus we see the proud woman, Eve, the disobedient man, Adam, and their disobedience regarding the tree of the knowledge of good and evil as the cause of the human predicament: Mankind was created good by God, but each of us is now disposed to sin and evil.

The consequences of the first sin are serious and immediate. It affects every member of the team for all eternity. Adam and Eve lost the gifts that God had conferred on them at creation. They lost the perfect use of reason and control over their passions. Guilt and shame entered their lives, as did, most serious of all, suffering and death. Yes, suffering and death, and every other calamity that befalls God's children, are consequences of sin.

Life on earth thus became spiritual warfare — a continuous struggle between the father of lies and his minions and the heavenly Father and his children of love, life, and truth. Like the long baseball season, the contest rages on hour after hour, day after day. There's an ongoing battle in the heavens among angels and devils, as well as a battle that rages here on earth, not only among enemies but in each person's heart.

Here is where the bat, the tree, and the cross come into play.

In the garden, the devil goes to the mound and overcomes our first parents. Every day the devil attempts to do the same to us. Satan is a very effective pitcher of lies, deceit, and confusion, and like Major League hurlers he is always plotting the downfall of the hitter. His goal is to take the bat out of our hands and render us impotent in the batter's box of life. And he does this everyday by the seven pitches he mastered, pitches in the form of temptations toward committing the seven capital sins.

The table on the following page shows seven types of pitches and the corresponding arsenal from the power of darkness.

The devil's first pitch is pride; a straight fastball right down the middle of a major human weakness. Satan can use it well, because it was the cause of his own fall from grace. Lucifer told God, "I will not serve." Pride is the sin that exalts our self-importance and blinds us to our need for God. When one's relationship with God is not right, neither is one's relationship with others. The proud person does not submit himself to God and his Church, but, like Eve, desires to know good and evil apart from God. One example of succumbing to this pitch of the devil is to claim to be spiritual with no need for "structured religion" or the Church. Deep down, this attitude makes way for inventing one's own morality (in order to engage in immorality), rejecting the Church's teaching on sexuality,

Pitcher's Arsenal	Devil's Arsenal
Fastball	Pride
Curve	Avarice
Cutter	Lust
Slider	Anger
Split Finger	Gluttony
Sinker	Envy
Change-up	Sloth

abortion, homosexual practice, euthanasia, etc.

The proud individual also has no use for holy Mass, devotions, or confession. I can pray to God in the park, or on the mountain, or by the ocean, this person proudly proclaims. There is no attempt to study closely the life of Jesus and understand his humility. Consequently, the soul strikes out, time after time, on the devil's fastball, and the person goes on living in a state of sin. Do these souls really expect to be called up to the big show in heaven without some serious work on hitting, teamwork, and humility?

The devil's second pitch is avarice; a curveball that fools the hitter into thinking what he has is good in itself. Avarice is selfishness manifested in a love for money and possessions. These goods are seen as ends in themselves and not as gifts that God has given to use to build his Church. Greed results in ignoring the biblical injunction to offer the first 10% of one's wealth to God. Instead of trusting in God and his provision, avarice results in the illusion of self-sufficiency and neglect of good works. Furthermore, this temptation is really a deceptive curveball, because it is the root of other sins and often misconstrued as a virtue. For example, hording wealth may be justified as making prudent plans for the future. The sin disrupts one's relationship with God because we worry more about what we have or what others may think. Dependence and trust in God are the paths to holiness, and one is called to be saint by imitating Christ in his sacrificial love. The devil throws the curveball temptation of self-gratification and catches us looking — at what we possess. God can read the heart and all gifts come from Him. "O LORD, thou wilt ordain peace for us, / thou has wrought for us all our works" (Is 26:12).

The devil's third pitch is lust; a cut fastball that he throws with a thousand and one variations. One only needs to be mildly observant to see how effective this satanic pitch is — almost unhittable. Modern Western culture has taken the sacred gifts of male and female sexuality, the holiness of marriage, and the exalted privilege of bearing children for the Kingdom and distorted each through the sin of lust into merely personal gratification. So many strikeouts result when we chase this pitch: abused women and children, destroyed families, broken bodies, tortured souls, implacable diseases, drug abuse, crime — the list goes on and on.

We live in a culture that constantly flaunts the human body in a degrading way, as manifested especially in pornography, most Hollywood films, popular music, advertising, politics, news reporting, and even education. Jesus in his sermon on the "mound" made it clear, "Blessed are the pure in heart, for they shall see God" (Mt 5:8).

Sexual sins are often associated with filth, and rightly so. Such sins committed with frequency cake over the doors and windows of the soul. The light of the Holy Spirit is completely obscured, and the soul is left in the darkness of its sexual perversions. In this state, it is not possible to see God. Blessed indeed are the clean of heart; they can see this pitch coming and avoid all the failures of swinging at this temptation.

The devil's fourth pitch is anger; hard-breaking stuff that

incites hate. The anger that Satan tempts one is not the justified variety (such as righteous anger at injustice). This temptation is rooted in hatred and revenge. The angry person is a destructive teammate, lacking charity in speech and action. The angry person destroys others by speech, using slander, detraction, or rash judgment (you should be able to define all three as a Major Leaguer on Our Lord's team). Or, he may destroy his neighbor by physical attacks or actions such as unjustified lawsuits. Most of all, the angry person holds grudges and can't forgive. This renders the person totally ineffective at life because he does not listen to or accept Our Lord's fundamental teaching on the nature of God himself. That teaching is of God's mercy and love. God is love. God forgives mortal sin no matter the sin committed, provided one confesses to a priest, is truly contrite for the sin, and makes a firm commitment to avoid the sin in the future. God not only forgives, but he forgets. In the Our Father, the Lord teaches us to pray: forgive us our trespasses as we forgive those who trespass against us. If one does not forgive, neither will one be forgiven. This is what we say when we pray each Our Father. It is a tough pitch to lay off, so listen to our heavenly coach and ask for the strength to succeed.

The devil's fifth pitch is gluttony; a very effective pitch thrown with the same motion as the fastball, but with excess movement. Gluttony is a sin of excess. This malady is characterized by eating or drinking to excess, even to the point of injuring one's health. Other manifestations are being too picky, accepting only the best or finest offerings, or demanding immediate gratification. The glutton's life is disordered because the body is given primacy over the soul. The glutton has no sense of disciplining his appetites and his body in order to become God's athlete — a holy person ready to do God's will. The individual seeks joy and happiness in serving the flesh and succumbs to the delight of the lower nature. He swings and misses the delights that come from his supernatural relationship with Christ. "Man shall not live by bread alone" (Mt 4:4), Our Lord told Satan while laying off Satan's pitch to turn stones into bread.

The devil's sixth pitch is envy, the sinkerball resentment or sadness at another's good fortune. Envy is not the same as jealousy. Jealously seeks another's advantage for oneself, while envy tries to destroy — or would like to destroy — another's advantage.

Jealousy can be good depending on what one is actually desiring. For example, being jealous of a coworker's computer skills can be a motivation for improvement.

Conversely, envy seeks harm, as in working to have a coworker demoted or terminated without cause, or simply because they appear to be in the way of one's own ambitions. Envy harms relationships because one is not satisfied with one's God-given abilities, success, or position. The devil thereby temps one to give in to discouragement, anger, and quarrels because of what one does not possess. By succumbing to envy, one squanders many at bats, leaving runners left on base when the acceptance of God's gifts could advance one in virtue while helping others to do so.

The devil's seventh pitch is sloth; a change-up that produces inertia. Here the temptation is to not exert or overwork oneself, especially in spiritual matters. Sloth is laziness when it comes to the things of God. Sloth tempts us to give our spiritual lives a minimum amount of effort or neglect our spirituality altogether. Maybe we still attend Sunday Mass, throw a dollar in the basket, and round up canned foods we are never going to use and donate them to the food pantry. One may even volunteer to help with a parish project or good work. But the slothful person avoids any sustained effort in prayer, visits to the Blessed Sacrament, attendance at daily Mass, regular Scripture reading, or studying to know and pass on the Faith. Rejecting these serious spiritual exercises because of difficulty or the effort required can be seriously sinful. This is the mediocre player, of whom Our Lord says in Revelation: "I know your works: you are neither cold nor hot. Would that you were either cold or hot! So, because you are lukewarm, and neither cold nor hot, I will spew you out of my mouth" (Rv 3:15–16). The devil discourages hustle in every way possible. Without some serious work, practicing Catholics who persist in this manner won't make it to the big show.

Thus does the devil take the bat out of our hands, rendering us incapable of driving in and scoring runs.

Christ now steps in and shows us the way to handle temptation and evil. He says, "Take up [your] cross and follow me" (Mt 16:24).

The bat also represents the cross, the instrument of Christ's victory. Satan's crafty pitching in the garden to our first parent's was undone by Christ's victory on Calvary. Here the proud woman, Eve, the disobedient man, Adam, and the tree give way to the humble woman Mary, the obedient man, Christ, and the cross. It was here that Satan watched our blessed Lord accept and take upon himself every evil the human race has ever and will ever commit. In doing so, the cross became the instrument of Our Lord's victory over sin and death. The Lord places that sacred wood in the hands of his teammates in the Catholic Church (again, "take up your cross and follow me"), and by it we can earn victory after victory.

Let's consider how Our Lord handles the evil one's offerings. To Satan's pitch of pride, the Lord said from the cross, "Father, into your hands I commit my spirit!" (Lk 23:46). Jesus suffers willingly the most horrible death ever devised by godless men. The Roman penalty of crucifixion was designed to inflict maximum pain for the maximum length of time. This is the death Jesus submitted to

Devil's Offering	Christ's Home Run
Pride	Father, into your hands I entrust my Spirit
Avarice	This day you shall be with me in paradise
Lust	Woman, behold your son; son behold your mother
Anger	Father, forgive them for they know not what they do

Gluttony	I thirst
Envy	My God, my God, why have thou forsaken me?
Sloth	It is finished

while wearing the crown of thorns, after being mocked mercilessly by those for whom he was dying. Could there be a more profound expression of humility and surrender?

In the Gospels there is only one thing Our Lord tells us to learn from him: "Take my yoke upon you, and learn from me; for I am gentle and lowly in heart" (Mt 11:29). Humility is the foundation of all virtues. God cannot coach us if we do not submit to his plan for us. Let us resolve to imitate our Savior's loving humility.

To Satan's pitch of avarice, Our Lord said from the Cross, to the good thief, "Truly, I say to you, today you will be with me in Paradise" (Lk 23: 43). The thieves were on the cross beside Our Lord because of avarice. They led a lifestyle built on the dirty business of theft. Now they were suffering the consequences. In the mystery of human freedom, one asked to be taken down so he could go on filling his life with trinkets. The other seized the moment to be taken up into paradise. The cross saved one, not the other. The Lord will not force himself on us. Hell is full of volunteers. Don't let the devil fool you with his curveball. The stuff in this life is passing…quickly.

To Satan's pitch of lust, Our Lord said from the cross, "Woman, behold your son! Then he said to the disciple, 'Behold, your mother'" (Jn 19:26–27). John was the only apostle at the foot of the cross. He was also the youngest disciple. Could this be a grace he was given because of his purity? After all, Mary, the Mother of God and the most honored person in humanity, was entrusted by Jesus to John's care. He would have to be pure to be given such a treasure by Jesus. But Mary was also given John as a son, and through John Jesus gave all of us to Mary. If Mary gave birth to Christ as a virgin at

Bethlehem in a miraculous manner; now, at the foot of the cross, in pain, she brings forth children in the Church. By her suffering, too, we are given birth in the life of grace through her only son. Let all men and woman have recourse to Mary most pure to protect them from all impurity. With the cross in hand, we can succeed in hitting this vicious pitch from Satan.

To Satan's pitch of anger, Our Lord said from the Cross, "Father, forgive them; for they know not what they do" (Lk 23:34). Anger dehumanizes a person; the throes of wrath obscure the divine image of God's love in the soul. Again, during the Sermon on the Mount, Jesus warns about evil thoughts. It is there that violence and revenge take root. The Major League follower of Christ would never condone repaying evil with evil, but strives to overcome evil with good. With pierced hands and feet and his scourged flesh exposed for all the world to see, Jesus offers tender words to his Father on behalf of his executioners. Jesus even makes an excuse for them: "for they know not what they do" (Lk 23:34). The successful hitter in the spiritual realm takes the cross into his hands and heart and expunges any idea of quarreling, bickering, backbiting, wrath, and revenge. In this way he learns to hit even Satan's most vicious slider, one even better than Phillies great Steve Carlton's in mowing down hapless hitters.

To Satan's pitch of gluttony, Our Lord said from the cross, "I thirst" (Jn 19:28). The glutton seeks not merely to satisfy but to sate the demands of his lower nature. The abuse of food and drink seems to be an easy and ready distraction; one "just this time" quickly gives way to another and another. Always the result is disappointment and discouragement, as we realize our lack of self-control and reliance on God's grace. This split-finger temptation from Satan always appears to be a strike and then falls out of the strike zone. It takes self-control and discipline to lay off this pitch. That is what the glutton lacks, and the devil exploits this weakness. Imagine the raging thirst Our Lord endured, exacerbated to an inhuman degree by the trauma of his wounds and the loss of so much blood. Yet, this divine utterance was not a complaint but a plea. Our blessed Lord's thirst cannot be slaked by a cup of water. What he desires most is the love of his teammates, those for whom he is dying. By his example our Savior teaches us that the cross — or self-renunciation — is the instrument to victory over the flesh. It proves our love when we discipline our bodies for the greater spiritual good of the team — his Church.

To Satan's pitch of envy, Our Lord said from the cross, "My God, my God, why have thou forsaken me?" (Mk 15:34). Satan's sinkerball draws the batter's eyes down and the result is pitches in the dirt that we either miss entirely or hit weakly as ground balls through the infield grass. Nothing uplifting happens when our focus is down on what others possess, accomplish, or achieve. The envious person cannot count his blessings; life always seems unfair, as if the person has been abandoned or overlooked.

Jesus' cry to his Father reveals that he suffered this dejection deeply, to the core of his human spirit. In this way Jesus knows what it is to suffer this separation from God and to place our focus on ourselves, pleasure, or science, and to live separated from the love of God and the healing power of the Church's sacraments. By these words Christ invites all to trust in his goodness and mercy. Take up the cross and abandon all forms of envy; rejoice in the knowledge that we are loved by so good a coach, mentor and Redeemer.

To Satan's pitch of sloth, Our Lord said from the cross, "It is finished" (Jn 19:30). The change-up may be the easiest pitch to throw, and here the temptation is to neglect good works or abandon projects started because of the discipline and effort required. Laziness and sensuality rob the player of full use of his talents. Think of the great ballplayers and consider the time and effort they spent training in order to be the very best. Consider the hours they devoted to hitting in the cage in the off-season, the extra batting practice they took during the season, and the time they committed to studying tendencies of opposing pitchers. Great players employ every possible means to gain a competitive advantage. It's called going the extra mile.

Now, our Savior could have redeemed us with just one drop of blood shed from his divine hand, so infinitely valuable was this offering from God become man. But Jesus was not satisfied with the minimum. To prove his love for us, He became "obedient unto death," as Saint Paul writes. Our Lord suffered in every member of his sacred flesh to an extreme degree. In the end, the soldier's spear opened the way to heaven, piercing Our Lord's side, releasing the last flood of blood and water. "It is finished," Our Lord said. His supreme act of love and self-giving was complete. Now his followers' life of love for God and their neighbors could begin. He puts the Major League uniform on us through baptism and places the cross into our hands and says, "Come be my disciple and follow me." Through the way of the cross we come to Christ's ultimate victory in the Resurrection. Indeed, "the bat" is the instrument of victory.

Remember how each bat is personalized for every player? Our heavenly Father also personalized the cross for our divine Savior. His crucifixion was long foretold by the prophets. The cross Jesus carried to the eternal plate is beautifully described by Archbishop Sheen whose cause for canonization is now underway. He writes:

> As a symbol of the world's rejection of his life-giving message, His enemies gave Him a cross, in which one bar is at variance with, or contradicts, the other: the horizontal bar symbolizing death (for all death is flat and prostrate), the vertical bar symbolizing life (for all life is upright and erect). But by a divine act, Our Lord made the sign of contradiction the sign of redemption and converted the cross into the crucifix. The Cross is the problem of pain and death, but the Crucifix is the solution. For when the God-man had ennobled it by His presence, He revealed that pain is the prelude to life, and unless we take up our own crosses and follow Him we cannot be His disciples. (*The Way of the Cross*, OSV, 1982)

Just as the Cross was prepared beforehand for Christ, the Father personalizes our bat or cross that we carry to the plate each day. We know this from the Gospel in which Jesus says, "Come to me, all who labor and are heavy laden, and I will give you rest. Take my yoke upon you, and learn from me; for I am gentle and lowly in heart, and you will find rest for your souls. For my yoke is easy, and my burden is light" (Mt 11:28–30). The reference to yoke would be known to His listeners as the harness worn by plow animals. A skilled yoke maker can fit the device to an individual animal, making the workload easier. You might say that like a bat is fitted and labeled with the name of the hitter, so the heavenly Father fashions an individual yoke of the cross for each of us. Like Our Lord, we take it up to the plate and live it out. The Catholic understands most deeply the significance of the bat in baseball, the tree at the Fall, and the cross in the plan of salvation.

Let's conclude where we started, with Ted Williams' quote: "Baseball is the only field of endeavor where a man can succeed three times out of ten and be considered a good performer." Ted's quote might have been taken from the Bible. Perhaps the author of the Book of Proverbs had this in mind when he wrote, "For a righteous man falls seven times, and rises again" (24:16). Also, to support Williams' assertion, in the New Testament Jesus said, "And if he sins against you seven times in the day, turns to you seven times, and says, 'I repent,' you must forgive him" (Lk 17:4). It is uncanny how directly hitting a baseball mirrors success in the spiritual life. Just as a hitter cannot get discouraged by striking out time after time, so we weak mortals must never succumb to discouragement.

We all know that hitters sometimes get into a slump. The best of hitters can walk away from the plate dozens of times without a single hit. Pitch after pitch, out after out, and game after game go by in failure. In the heat of competition, discouragement sets in, which make the problem worse. Discouragement is always the enemy. Second-guessing, anger, and frustration are never the answer to overcoming a slump. It is always to return to fundamentals, additional practice in the batting cage, coaching instruction, building confidence. Often the result is newfound hitting prowess.

Likewise, the saints could experience slumps just like hitters do. God seems distant if not absent altogether. Prayer is difficult, if not downright painful, and spiritual reading dry. That's Satan pitching discouragement. He constantly wants us to believe we can't possibly perform the way God wants; goodness is not for us, look at the other person's misbehavior; be satisfied with mediocrity. The tenacious ballplayer overcomes slumps through persistence and hard work. No less is demanded in becoming a spiritual pro.

Our fallen human nature is prone to weakness, and we will strike out, pop up, and hit into double plays where we cause others to sin. Here humility is especially needed in the confessional. Mercy and forgiveness are given through the priest from God through the blood of Christ. Enough coaching in the confessional and making swings of virtue in the spiritual batting cage and our batting average will improve. With prayer and sacrifice, it is possible to become a .400 hitter. Then when we step into the batter's box of life, Satan will say, "Darn, he's up!"

—

QUESTIONS FOR REFLECTION – THE INTENTIONAL WALK

⚾ BALL ONE

Do I believe in the real existence of the devil, or have I bought into the cultural lie that the devil, and consequently hell, is not real?

⚾ BALL TWO

What is my attitude to the cross and suffering? Do I see the Church's beautiful teaching about the infinite value of suffering as means of saving souls and saving others? Do I understand that when God gives me a cross, he in putting the bat into my hands as a means to get home and drive others in?

⚾ BALL THREE

Do I get easily discourage by my faults and repeated failures of falling into the same sins? Do I realize at that moment God's infinite mercy will help to continue fighting, and that with his grace I can overcome all sin with time, effort, and recourse to the sacraments?

⚾ BALL FOUR

Great hitters put extraordinary effort and time to improve their skills as the saints invested extraordinary effort and time in prayer. Do I give God the first and best time in prayer? Do I seek to show my love for Jesus by faithfulness in prayer even when it is most difficult? Is my prayer life increasing my union with Our Lord, or is it superficial?

—ON DECK—

Ven. Fulton J. Sheen

"There are millions and millions of favors hanging from heaven on silken cords, and prayer is the sword that cuts them."

6TH INNING

The Seasons

For everything there is a season, and a time for every matter under heaven. — Eccclesiastes 3:1

People ask me what I do in winter when there's no baseball. I'll tell you what I do. I stare out the window and wait for spring.
— Rogers Hornsby

It is stunning how baseball's cycle of a full season mirrors creation's. Not coincidentally, the Church's calendar follows a similar cyclical rhythm. Let's explore how to enjoy and profit each year from the "three" seasons: nature's, baseball's, and the liturgical seasons'.

"Spring is sprung, the grass is riz, / I wonder where the baseball is ..." may just be a better take on the old poem written by Anonymous. The cosmic clock ordains that come spring daylight hours lengthen, winter freeze dissipates, and blossoms appear. At the same time, players report for spring training. Thus begins a season of new life in nature, and correspondingly baseball, as teams begin to prepare for opening day.

What follows is the long hot summer, and with it the long slog through the sport's most demanding season. Nature is in full bloom and Church takes us through Ordinary Time.

Then as the daylight hours grow shorter nature unfolds a last colorful show. Baseball's best engages in the thrilling postseason championship chase, while the Church directs our vision to the glow of divine glory, celebrating the feasts of All Souls, All Saints, and culminating in the feast of Christ the King on the last Sunday of the Church year.

Finally, in winter, as nature goes cold and silent, the bats and balls are idle and put aside to sleep. While weary arms recover, the Church announces the penitential season of Advent before the winter chill and night is dispelled with the birth of the newborn King. Christmas comes celebrating the gift of divine majesty to the human race — and a time to receive bats, balls, and gloves from Santa.

We start our season review with spring! Legendary pitcher Whitey Ford once said of spring training, "The way to make coaches think you are in shape in the spring is to get a tan." That may be sufficient for the proven veterans whose place on the team is a lock, but most players report to spring training with something to prove. The blossoms, the buds on the trees, and sunshine are there to enjoy, but training properly requires work and effort. The challenge of a new season and its promise beckons. We'll get 'em this year!

Spring, spring training, and the liturgical season of Lent occur relatively at the same time. In fact, the Teutonic origin of the word "Lent" means spring.

Lent's spiritual origins, however, are found in Jesus' forty days and forty nights of fasting and prayer before beginning his public ministry. Thus as the blossoms arrive, and pitchers and catchers are the first to report to camp, the faithful Catholic receives ashes on Ash Wednesday.

As Major Leaguers begin training for opening day, Catholics prepare or train, so to speak, for celebrating the Resurrection — opening day to eternal life! There are no coincidences in the divine economy. Catholics can enjoy nature's spring blossoming, follow their team in the Grapefruit or Cactus League, and pray, fast, and give alms during spiritual spring training. What is not to love?

Then comes opening day. Each team gets a fresh start, with a retooled roster and a blank slate. The best pitcher for each team, its ace, takes the mound.

The experienced fan pays more attention to what happens throughout the season's first week than winning or losing on opening day. The first week is a better indicator of the season ahead, as the starting rotation shows its strength (or weakness) and hitters begin to get comfortable. The first eight days provide the opportunity to become familiar with a new lineup and any managerial changes.

About this time, the Catholic concludes Lent and celebrates Christ's passion during Holy Week, especially the last three days, called the Triduum. The preeminent liturgy of the Triduum presents the Last Supper, Crucifixion, and Resurrection over what, in its essence, is a single three-day service. The Triduum concludes with the Easter Vigil, where the darkness of Lent is dispelled and the Light of Christ bursts forth. **Christ is risen!**

Then Easter is celebrated as an octave — that is, the Easter Mass is celebrated for eight days to rejoice in the Lord's resurrection, the central tenet and foundation of the Catholic Faith. Catholics are renewed for a fresh start — again a spiritual opening day. In fact, Easter is celebrated for fifty days in the liturgical calendar. Thus the longest liturgical season kicks off at the same time as the lengthy baseball season.

Then we come to the baseball season and a time in the Church calendar called Ordinary Time. Tom Trebelhorn, when managing the Milwaukee Brewers years ago, said, "Baseball has got to be fun, because if it is not fun, it's a long time to be in agony." Major League teams play a 162-game schedule. Major League Baseball's thirty teams will take the field a collective 2,430 times over the course of six months. It is a long, grueling season that, of course, mimics life's vicissitudes. If you are winning, it is fun; but losing brings with it the longing for the season to end. The wins and losses are only part of it. Major League players' records are on the line and each game counts to build toward that player's legacy. That is why Micky Mantle, looking back, said, "During my 18 years I came to bat almost 10,000 times. I struck out about 1,700 times and walked maybe 1,800 times. You figure a ballplayer will average about five hundred at bats a season. That means I played seven years without ever hitting the ball."

Day after day, inning after inning, and game after game,

individual and team stats are established. Batting averages go up and down, errors accumulate, home runs and strike outs are counted. The great, the good, the bad, and the ugly unfold as careers wax and wane. The great players exhibit the intensity that leads to excellence. Think of Pete Rose running full speed down to first base after a walk; Andre Dawson during his MVP season in right field for the Cubs banging into a wall to make a catch in the late innings of an 11-1 victory; or Steve Carlton piling up strikeouts for a hapless Phillies team. Whatever the outcome, each opportunity for hitting, pitching, or fielding finds its way into the record books. It all counts; it's all tallied in the definitive book of baseball records. Baseball has long been considered the most stats obsessed of all sports — perhaps because data presents the only way to keep track of such a vast experience.

Ordinary time in the new liturgical calendar for the Catholic is like the 162-game season. It is called "ordinary" not because it is common, but because the weeks of Ordinary Time are numbered. The Latin word *ordinalis*, which refers to numbers in a series, stems from the Latin word *ordo*, from which we get the English word *order*. Thus the numbered weeks of Ordinary Time represent the ordered life of the Church — the period in which we live our lives neither in feasting (as in the Christmas and Easter seasons) or in more severe penance (as in Advent and Lent), but in watchfulness and expectation of the Second Coming of Christ.

It is in Ordinary Time especially that the spiritual minded Catholic deepens his love for God and others. Every act of kindness is a hit, an act of forgiveness a home run, bringing a friend to mass an RBI, leading a soul back to the Church is a definite win. Correspondingly, an act of revenge means we've struck out, a cross word is an error, and an act of impurity a loss. All will be recorded in the Book of Life and examined on judgment day.

Before the seasons (all three) converge at the end, there is a midsummer celebration. Spring turns into the dog days of summer, and summer brings the All Star break and the feast of Saint John the Baptist. As the Major Leaguers showcase their best in the mid-season classic, so does the Church.

In late June, the birthday of John the Baptist is celebrated. The Church calendar contains only three birthdays: Jesus, born in perfect humanity without original sin; Mary, conceived without original sin in anticipation of the death of her son; and John the Baptist, sanctified in Elizabeth's womb during Mary's visit.

We celebrate Mary's privilege of being conceived without sin on December 8, the feast of the Immaculate Conception. This feast is nine months before we celebrate Mary's birth on September 8. Other than Jesus, Mary is the only person that the Church has declared definitively to be born without original sin (also conceived as such). There's a long-held belief, however, that as a result of John the Baptist being sanctified in his mother's womb that he, too, entered the world without the taint of original sin (although not conceived as such). That's why the feast days of Jesus, Mary, and John the Baptist occur on their birthdays — at the time of their union with God. For all other saints, we celebrate the date of their death as the memorial of their entrance into glory. He of whom Jesus said, "Among those born of woman none is greater than John" (Lk 7:28).

Notice one more connection, however, with the boys of summer. John's birth is celebrated in June when the daylight begins to decrease. This will continue until winter comes at Christmastime when we celebrate the birthday of Our Lord and daylight begins to increase. Beautiful poetry when you consider that John said, "He must increase, but I must decrease" (Jn 3:30). The spiritually-minded ballplayer reflects at the All Star break not so much on his own role in life, for that is not our final reward. The reward is Jesus Christ who must increase; for him all four seasons exist.

No doubt God gave us the four seasons to take the weariness of time away. The best proof of this is the fall, during which we experience nature's brilliant show of colors and baseball's brilliant play of the playoffs. It is a splendid time of year for the Church as well, recalling our ultimate destiny. The League Championships Series and the World Series put the final teams on the field for baseball's version of an octave: a seven-game series. All of the planning, preparation, and performances from spring training on culminate in the final eight wins it takes to become world champions. There is nothing else to distract the committed fan from the season's statistics, strategies, and performances which are part of the analysis of how the final drama may play out. It captures the fans serious attention. Only one champion will be crowned. Then it's over — forever — never to be repeated.

At the same time, the Church presents to the faithful the culmination of the liturgical year in November with the month of the Holy Souls — those suffering in purgatory and the triumphant in heaven. The liturgical year ends with the crowning of our champion — Christ the King. Here the faithful Catholic recalls that the King wears a crown of thorns and reigns not from a throne but from the cross. Our king reminds us on this feast that the cross leads to the Resurrection and a new season in eternity. It also reminds the fans that Christ the King will come as judge. In this sense, the Church puts forth the reminder that our careers are short and the four last things merit our serious attention. The four last things are death, judgment, heaven, and hell. Recall Jesus words: "For what does it profit a man, to gain the whole world and forfeit his life?" (Mk 8:36). We will consider these ultimate realities in greater depth in a chapter to come.

——

QUESTIONS FOR REFLECTION - THE INTENTIONAL WALK

 BALL ONE

Do I see time as a gift from God with one purpose: to grow in Major League holiness? Do I make good use of my time, giving the first and best time of the day to prayer?

BALL TWO

Am I willing to train as hard as a professional athlete to accomplish spiritual growth? Do I have a plan to rid myself of sin as the season moves along, desiring to rack up wins against my weaknesses?

BALL THREE

Do I have a plan to take full spiritual advantage of the penitential seasons of Lent and Advent? Do I realize that, like spring training, God lavishes these special times with grace for us to grow in holiness?

BALL FOUR

Do I recognize and appreciate the beauty of the seasons and that the liturgical calendar's purpose is to renew and deepen my faith and love for Christ? Do I live it intensely?

—ON DECK—

Bishop Louis Laravoire Marrow

"At the beginning of the four seasons—spring, summer, Autumn, Fall—the Ember Days are celebrated to implore God's blessings on the fruit of the earth; those days are likewise intended as special occasions for praying for the clergy. The Ember Days are the Wednesdays Fridays and Saturdays following December 13th, the first Sunday of Lent, Pentecost, and September 14th. Ordinations take place on Ember Saturdays. Ember Days are days of prayer, fasting and abstinence." (*My Catholic Faith*, My Mission House, 1949)

7TH INNING

The Stadium and the Cathedral

For zeal for thy house has consumed me. — Psalm 69:9

The foul poles at Houston Astros Minute Maid Park reflect a labor of love. Each screen on the poles contains an image that reflects a family's devotion to the game of baseball. Napoleon Thibodeau, a lifelong Boston Red Sox fan, has his name engraved on the right field foul pole screen. His sons' family names are on the screen of the left field foul pole.

Two of Napoleon's sons, Tim and Tom, ended up in the contracting business in Houston. When the stadium broke ground on October 30, 1997, Tom's company, Stature Commercial Construction, won the contract to install the concrete bases for the foul poles as well as the retaining walls for the infamous short-porch Crawford boxes in left field.

At the time, Tim's company had not yet been contracted to do the foul poles, and Napoleon was still living and proud of the work his sons were doing, even though he was a Red Sox devotee. He passed away August 12, 1998, during the construction of the stadium.

Shortly after, Tim's company, Aber Fence, Inc., was awarded the contract to fabricate and install all the fencing at Minute Maid Park, which included the bullpens and all exterior fencing (back then the stadium was named Enron Field). The actual name of the construction project was The Ballpark at Union Station. Specifically, Tim's contract included the fabrication and installation of the metal screens attached to the side (fair side) of the foul poles.

As Tim relates, "I wanted to pay tribute to my father who passed away a little over a year before the foul poles were installed." He explains the fabrication process: "We welded pad eyes to the actual poles so then we could bolt the screens to the poles. I then used a hand engraver and etched Napoleon's name on the screens that were to be installed on the right-field pole. I was the only person to know that I did this." Tim continued, "After I engraved his name, I preserved it with primer. I did the same thing to the left-field screens, but this time I engraved the name of my family: my name, Tim; Sandi, my wife; son Timmy Jr.; and daughter Megan," he declared.

The foul-pole installation was a stated milestone for the project, and it was covered by local news channels. Said Tim, "I cannot tell you how proud I was watching that on TV. Major League Baseball was at the installation to oversee the entire event." He concluded with, "I know one thing, I could feel the presence of my father in my heart the day those poles were erected."

There on the foul-pole screens in Minute Maid Park is one family's special connection to each other in life and death and to the game they love.

Like holy sites, ballparks are sometimes a place of pilgrimage. One of my uncles made it his mission to visit and take a picture in every Major League park (he was also a faithful Catholic and would always visit churches and shrines as well). Year after year he would plan vacations and trips around the next stadium visit. Each park has its own mystique and magic, he would say. But it is not just viewing a game in a different stadium that matters to the serious fan. My uncle would be upset if you asked him to rank each park according to superficial considerations such as food, locations, views, mascots, music, beer selection, etc. He understood the ballparks impact on the game itself and could see and enjoy aspects of a ballpark the superficial fan could not.

Take one example of a ballpark's influence on the game. The field's dimensions can determine the complexion of a pitching staff. Casey Stengel notoriously would not pitch the great Whitey Ford in Boston's Fenway Park. Casey avoided the left-hander's clash with right-hand hitters because of the looming green monster and short left-field dimension. This proved to be sound managing as Ford, who had a lifetime ERA lower than Sandy Koufax, registered a lifetime ERA of 6.16 in his few starts at Fenway. One can conclude that left-handed hitters playing home games in Boston will face left-handers far less frequently. To this day, the Red Sox are less prone to load up the pitching staff with southpaws than say the Yankees, who play in the more spacious environs in the Bronx. The astute fan sees the game in this deeper relief.

The baseball faithfuls' affinity with stadiums, as in the case of Tim Thibodeau and my uncle, is not hard to understand. It is where the drama of the national pastime unfolds in the constant rhythm of excellence. The stadium is impressive in its proportions and distinctive features. It houses memorials to its team's greatest players; pennants of championships adorn the facades; and each park offers its unique dimensions, playing-field features, quirks, aromas, and sounds. So much the same, but so very different — that might be the way to describe the experience of taking in a game at various parks. Then there are the memories of significant victories, agonizing losses, great plays, and shattered records.

Even stadiums that have been razed and gobbled up in urban development live on with memorials of their own. Think of the Pittsburgh's Forbes Field left-field-wall portion that still stands on the University of Pittsburgh campus marking Bill Mazeroski's seventh-game winning homer in the 1960 World Series, or the marker in south Atlanta, site of Hank Aaron's 715th home run, breaking Babe Ruth's career record. Pictures of stadiums abound in offices, workshops, and restaurant all across America. Little expense is spared when building new stadiums destined to become hallowed grounds.

Stadiums, like churches, bring the community together. Spectators come and align themselves in neat rows to take in a game and enjoy the atmosphere. They focus their attention on the field, watching the nine-inning drama play out. Will something that happens today be remembered as part of a player's destiny?

One might say the game unfolds like a liturgy. Here is where baseball and Catholicism offer the initiated a fulfilling mystical experience. To the thoughtful, passionate, and engaged fan, baseball offers a satisfying experience of athletic competition, a noble exercise that engages all the senses. This is the draw and magnetism of the game. It is why umpire Bill Klem can say, "Baseball is more than a game to me, it is a religion."

Perhaps Bart Giamatti, who was the president of Yale University and left that lofty position in academia for baseball's top office as commissioner, expressed it best when he said, "There are a lot of people who know me who can't understand for the life of them why I would go to work on something as unserious as baseball. If they only knew." Indeed, baseball is very serious; it's an indispensable part of our culture, identity, and national conversation. Is this not precisely why this great game can lead us to a deeper relationship with the Catholic Church: one presents a serious approach to life, the other a most serious approach to eternal life.

Now let's switch to another world, even more majestic, noble, and enduring than baseball. We contemplate the mysteries of the Catholic Church as found in the great cathedrals and churches present on every continent. Like the foul poles lifting our eyes to heaven, our church's spires and steeples soar in prayer.

The baseball fanatic and the passionate Catholic have the best of both worlds — "cathedrals" that house a multitude of meanings. Of course, baseball, as attractive as it is, pales in comparison. Worldly pursuits cannot fill the human desire for love and meaning. This can only come from God who made us for himself. As St. Augustine put it, "You have made us for yourself, O Lord, and our heart is restless until it rests in you." Great are you, O Lord, and exceedingly worthy of praise; your power is immense.

Let's consider the immense importance of the Church's structures in our quest for love and eternal happiness.

My father-in-law, Wayne Smith, and mother-in-law, Ruth Smith, retired to Port Charlotte, Florida. As converts, they became devout Catholics. Each did everything they could to help in their new parish, St. Charles Borromeo. They also became Texas Rangers fans, attending spring-training games in Port Charlotte; baseball was important but secondary.

When it came time for the church to be renovated, they stepped forward to make a donation for a stained-glass window that depicts the Seventh Station of the Cross: Jesus Falls the Second Time. The window was donated as a memorial for the Smith family. It was Wayne and Ruth's wish that the family would benefit from the prayers said for the church's benefactors. They also wanted those who would come after to experience the beauty and joy of the church and be led to a greater love for God and neighbor.

Wayne and Ruth's act of love has been repeated countless times through the centuries. Every church has been built through the generous gifts of the faithful. This is how, on an earthly level, the Catholic Church has given the world incomparable marvels of beauty and architecture in her cathedrals around the world. For centuries, churches and pilgrimage sites have been built and preserved by Catholic dioceses and Catholic orders — from the humblest to the most famous. This includes St. Peter's Basilica, the world's largest church on Palatine Hill in Rome, site of St. Peter's upside-down crucifixion and burial; St. Paul Outside the Walls, also in Rome at the site of Paul's martyrdom; the church on the site of the Sermon on the Mount; and the Church of All Nations in the Garden of Gethsemane in the Holy Land.

Then there are the major shrines, which have often been built at the request of the Blessed Mother through her apparitions. Lourdes may be the most famous — a site of so many miraculous cures. There is also the Fátima Shrine in Portugal. Our Lady of Guadalupe in Mexico contains the miraculously imprinted seer Juan Diego's *tilma* (outer garment) with her image, which inexplicably remains impervious to the ravages of time. It remains on perpetual display at the site where the Blessed Mother asked that a church be built. Then there are the numerous parish churches and local shrines dotting the landscape all over the world. As stadiums beckon to fans, so churches reach out to the faithful.

One point of digression here when speaking of the parallels between stadiums and churches: We spend untold tax dollars on stadiums, sparing no expense to outdo rival cities. Yet there is often a cry of protest that arises against the building or remodeling of our churches.

Let's look at it from the perspective of keeping one's priorities in proper order. In the hierarchy of values, the Gospel reminds us that God is first, our neighbor is second, then we are third, and baseball assumes whatever importance it has in that context. That ranking of priorities should govern every aspect of our life. God, others, self — to repeat, God, others, self. When we invert these priorities, we diminish our opportunities for holiness and tarnish relationships with Our Lord and others (the team). To put God first means we offer the best of our time, talent, and treasure. Our treasure is required to build the places of worship that will offer the Church future popes, priests, husbands and wives, and saints who will care for the Kingdom.

We learn about extravagance towards God in the Gospel:

And while he was in Bethany in the house of Simon the leper, as he sat at table, a woman came with an alabaster jar of ointment of pure nard, very costly, and she broke the jar and poured it over his head. But there were some who said to themselves indignantly, "Why was the ointment thus wasted? For this ointment might have been sold for more than three hundred denarii, and given to the poor." And they reproached her. But Jesus said, "Let her alone; why do you trouble her? She has done a beautiful thing for e. For you will always have the poor with you, and whenever you will, you can do good to them; but you will not always have me. She has done what she could; she has anointed my body beforehand for burying. And truly, I say to you, wherever the gospel is preached in the whole world, what she has done will be told in memory of her."

Then Judas Iscariot, who was one of the twelve, went to the chief priests in order to betray him to them. And when they heard it they were glad, and promised to give him money. And he sought an opportunity to betray him. (Mark 14:3–10)

The woman, at great sacrifice, lavished on Our Lord her most expensive perfume. It was a gift of love and a gesture that showed God was first in her life. The cynics who saw this only in terms of money considered it a waste. They hid their self-righteousness behind their so-called concern for the poor. Jesus rebukes them and praises the woman for doing good to him. Jesus tells them, essentially, the woman has her priorities in order, giving the best to God. Jesus tells them tersely, "You can give to the poor anytime you want, so why haven't you?" Notice how those who profess concern for the poor usually do so with others' money or possessions?

So often, Catholics will say that the Church should sell off its priceless art and other treasures and give them to the poor. This inverts Gospel priorities. God deserves not only the very best perfume but the finest architectural and interior design and art in our places of worship. Nothing shows more to the world that Our Lord is first than the houses we build for him. Second, it is not the Church's art to give away. The benefactors (like Wayne and Ruth) contributed for the edification of future generations.

The work of Michelangelo in the Sistine Chapel continues to inspire hearts to love God and, consequently, to help the poor. If all the Church's possessions were sold, some poor would be helped. But we would have shortchanged Our Lord. The poor would still be with us, and we would all be poorer, too.

Have you ever heard anyone say we should sell the city's

baseball stadium to help the poor?

The thoughtful, engaged, and passionate Catholic appreciates the wonders of our places of worship. We have ornate sanctuaries, with beautiful paintings and murals of Bible scenes, as well as stained glass windows depicting the mysteries of Our Lord's life; we have statues honoring saints (Hall of Fame greats), from Stephen, the first martyr, to our contemporary, Pope St. John Paul II. Then there are the sensory expressions of beauty: candles, flowers, incense, bells, and music (a bonus if pipe organs fill the ears with its intensity). And in all cases, there is the crucifix — in every church, the crucifix: that torturous yet elegant reminder of God's love for his children, as it represents the central mystery of redemption. Our churches provide much to contemplate about the richness of salvation history and ones' personal destiny. Where else will you find that?

But architecture, whether it be the most magnificent (such as Notre Dame in Montreal) or the humblest country church, is really secondary. Here again we turn to the Eucharist. The stupendous aspect of each Catholic Church is that OUR BLESSED LORD IS PRESENT! Yes, Christ is found in his Church, really truly present in the tabernacle: Body and Blood, Soul and Divinity. A visitor to a church will notice, either in the sanctuary or a side chapel, the tabernacle, beside which a red-glass-encased candle will be burning indicating that Our Lord is physically present.

The Real Presence of Christ in the tabernacle is the single most important tenet of the Catholic Faith. Our Lord Jesus gives himself, so fragile and helpless, in the form of bread for love of his children. Jesus, whose heart beats faster in love when you walk into a Church. Jesus, who wants so desperately your love! He's really there!

This is why many faithful will bow and bless themselves when they pass a church. Others will stop in to pay a visit to Our Lord. Some will spend an hour as Jesus asked Peter, James, and John to do in the Garden.

Catholic churches are the most sacred spaces on earth. Given this thought, the structure of the church building itself takes on new meaning. It is precisely why my uncle would make pilgrimages to churches on his trips to stadiums. He found baseball everywhere he went, but first he found Christ in the church; visiting Christ outranked in importance, by far, his baseball attendance. Baseball is of insignificant consequence when compared to the mysteries of the Faith.

For the Catholic who loves the Faith, the tabernacle is the window to heaven. It is the most wondrous attraction on the face of the earth. With the Psalmist let us pray, "Zeal for [your] house has consumed me."

How can it be that we can easily spend three hours plus watching a ball game, but balk at giving Our Lord one hour a week attending Mass? Or spending one hour praying in his Eucharistic presence before our church's tabernacle?

Time for a priority check, don't you think?

— —

QUESTIONS FOR REFLECTION - THE INTENTIONAL WALK

BALL ONE

Like a properly attired Major League player, does my behavior, attitude, dress, and example reflect my love and reverence due to the House of God and the Blessed Sacrament present there for me?

BALL TWO

Do I take the time to reflect on the treasure contained in the tabernacle in each Catholic church — Jesus himself? Do I point this out to my children (grandchildren) and others?

BALL THREE

Do I contribute time, talent, and treasure to beautify and support my parish church?

BALL FOUR

Do I make time to participate in devotions, programs, and evangelizing opportunities to be a good teammate and help drive in runs for the Kingdom?

—ON DECK—

Edwin Benson (in "The Architecture That Feeds the Soul," at Return to Order website)

"Some modern voices may cry out, 'How can you justify all this opulence when the hungry are all around us?' The answer is as simple as it is profound. We are all hungry and it is the hunger of the soul. We are hungry for the true, the good, the beautiful. Praise God for those who design, built and preserve those beautiful places in which our souls can be fed."

8TH INNING

Rules, Rules, Rules

If you love me, you will keep my commandments. — John 14:15

Bart Giamatti had an intense love for the game of baseball. He was not only Major League Baseball's commissioner briefly before his untimely death in 1989, but he was also one of the more eloquent spokesmen for the game. The former president of Yale University, who left that position for his baseball post, said, "Baseball has the largest library of law and love and custom and ritual, and therefore, in a nation that fundamentally believes it is a nation under law, well, baseball is America's most privileged version of the level field." Bart believed that fans looked to games for a "stable artifice," an island of clear rules and of predictable government in an ever-changing world. More than government or politics, baseball offers unparalleled lessons in ethics and morality due to its long and scrupulous examination of right behavior. Baseball's rules and traditions make up this legacy. It is here also that baseball can lead to moral clarity in the spiritual realm. Let's have a look.

No game has as many rules as baseball — so many that the game might be said to have its own catechism. The pdf version of the rule book has over 130 pages of regulations, followed by a stream of definitions. Rules govern the delicate balance of the field, the ball, the bats, runs, outs, pitching, catching, running, throwing, and hitting. Such rules were established decades ago and remain unchanged. In fact, there have been very few changes in the last century that one can say radically impacted the game since its inception.

The first may be the 1910 rule that allowed a cork center to be added to the baseball. Then, in 1920, both leagues began using balls with yarn made from Australia. The stronger yarn could be wound tighter and this material ushered in the "live ball era."

In 1959, Major League Baseball set minimum fence dimensions for new parks at 325-400-325 (that's left-field line/ center field/right-field line). Two most recent rules of impact were adopted in 1969 after the infamous 1968's "year of the pitcher," when overall batting averages reached their nadir at .237 (lowest ever). In response, the pitcher's mound was lowered five inches (the previous fifteen-inch mound height was adopted in 1904), and the strike zone height was reduced to the armpits to right above the knees. Finally, in 1973, the American League adopted the controversial-to-this-day rule permitting the designated hitter, forever offending the baseball "purists."

Rarely in this age of sport are the essential rules left undisturbed for so long. A spectator from the early 1900s would not feel like an alien in a modern ballpark. The essentials of the game remain intact, thus assuring order, stability, excellence, and the essential connection from one generation to another among fans and players. Indeed, the defining elements of baseball cannot be changed without severe distortion, which would render the game unrecognizable. For instance, put the bases 92 feet apart, or 88, instead of the standard 90, and those bang-bang plays at first on infield grounders disappear.

No one would argue that the rules are superfluous, burdensome, or outdated. As in any endeavor there must be objectivity and tranquility. This corresponds to the natural order. Baseball, in this sense, is a microcosm of the cosmos. The rules establish the immutable truth. The umpires — mere humans as they are — take great pains to enforce the statutes evenly, but they do bring an element of subjectivity that is often the source of error and controversy. They must make judgment calls in addition to applying the rules in all situations.

As former longtime umpire Bill Klem noted, regarding

balls and strikes, "They ain't nothing until I call 'em." Finally, the commissioner acts as a one-man Supreme Court interpreting whether a law has been properly applied.

Then there are rules that require counsel from a baseball canon lawyer in order to understand how each came to be. The following is an example: If a player pinch hits for a batter in the middle of an at bat with two strikes and strikes out, the at bat and strikeout are credited to the replaced batter. Any other outcome is credited to the pinch-hitter.

Or how about this gem? There are two strikes on the batter, and a runner attempts to steal home, and the pitch hits the runner in the strike zone, the batter is out. The run does not score if there are two outs; if there are less than two outs, it does.

Arcane rules like these may not seem at first blush to be fair or logical, but they do provide for harmony and good order. Plus, we can learn some timeless principles from baseball situations evoking the rule book. Here are three.

The need for baseball's complex rules was never more evident than on the night of April 21, 2013, in Milwaukee. Brewers shortstop Jean Segura was out three times on one play while attempting to steal third, but still ended safely (according to the umpires) back on first when all the chaos was over. You have to see it to believe it; the play can be accessed on You Tube entitled *Segura's Baserunning Adventures*, and watching it will help you understand the following.

That Friday night, Segura was on second with Ryan Braun on first. Segura broke from second base to steal third. Chicago pitcher Shawn Camp saw him break for third and threw to third. Caught in a rundown with third baseman Luis Valbuena chasing him, Segura dove safely into second. At the same time Braun arrived at second from first. (At this point, Braun should have been out, because there can't be two runners on the same base, and the first runner to have gained the base safely has the right to return to it.) Valbuena in rapid succession tagged both runners and then tagged Segura a second time when he gets up to leave the base. (When Segura left the base voluntarily and was tagged, he should have been called out.) Braun quickly and correctly was called out, and a confused Segura, who was safe and entitled to second base with no reason to leave, did not realize Braun was the one being called out (not him). Segura heads off the field (at least for the first few steps after leaving second).

But Segura's first-base coach, Garth Iorg, alertly realizes Segura was not called out, and at Iorg's promptings, Segura runs back to first, chased by the Cubs' Darwin Barney who took the ball from Valbuena. Segura reaches first base safely after the chase. He then starts to leave the field from first base still thinking he was out when he was constrained by Iorg. He should have been ruled out, however, for running the base paths in reverse order. Once you get to second base or third base safely, you can't go back to second or first.

When the mess was sorted out, Segura was ruled safe at first — again, while Braun, who started the play at first, was out. It all happened so fast umpires, players, and even the fans could not quickly sort out the confusion to understand what had transpired.

It had been a long time since any player in Major League Baseball reversed bases. In fact, the last time was over a century before. On August 4, 1911, Washington Senator Germany Schaefer stole first base with the intention to steal second — again to allow a runner on third a chance to steal home on the throw to second. That play ended in failure but resulted in a rule change. In 1920, reverse base running was proscribed. Rule 7.08i stipulates that after a runner reaches a base, he is out if he runs the bases in reverse order for the purpose of confusing the defense or making a travesty of the game. Clearly, that is not what Segura did, so in the heat of things that was not the call. The umpires, however, missed three opportunities on the play to call Segura out: when he was tagged leaving first, when he abandoned second to leave the field, and when the coach physically restrained him from leaving first.

Stuart Miller, in a 2013 article in *The New York Times* sorts it all out. He writes about the one-runner triple play executed against Segura that night that was not called. Accordingly, Rule 701 applies here mandating that if a runner legally acquires title to a base, and the pitcher assumes his pitching position, the runner may not return to a previously occupied base. According to that rule, Segura was out. Furthermore, Rule 7.08a can be cited which states a runner is deemed to be out by abandoning his efforts to run the bases. Finally, a coach touching an active runner on the bases is consider an illegal assist and the runner is automatically out.

When play resumes Segura was on first — again — with two out. He attempted to steal second for the second time in the inning. After surviving the triple jeopardy, he was thrown out at second, concluding perhaps the strangest inning in modern baseball; it was over where it began, the Cubs leading 5-4.

In this instance the rules were in place to make the correct determination. Human error is never a reason to invalidate a law or excuse wrong activity. It is never acceptable to say that the outcome should be whatever the umpire decided. The objective moral order dictates **right is right and wrong is wrong**. More on this later.

The strange odyssey of Segura around the bases fortunately had no impact on the final outcome of the game. Had it, a protest may have been filed and, upon objective review, the play may have been overturned. The next example shows the proper application of the law.

Another challenge to baseball doctrine and its "pastoral application" occurred in the infamous Pine Tar Game. On July 24, 1983, the Royals were playing the Yankees in New York. The Royals were down 4-3 with two outs in the ninth. With U. L. Washington on first, George Brett hit a home run to give the Royals the lead 5-4.

Yankee manager Billy Martin then conferred with the home-plate umpire, Tim McClelland, as well as his crew, pointing out that Brett's bat had an inordinate amount of pine tar on it and up the handle, contrary to baseball rules. After a long inspection of the bat and measuring the location of the pine tar against the width of home plate, McClelland pointed to Brett and signaled out. With the home run nullified the game was over. Brett exploded in protest to no avail.

The Royals protested the game and four days later American League President Lee MacPhail overturned the umpire's decision.

The umpires correctly applied baseball's rule, as it was written. As enumerated in a Wikipedia article on the subject, rule 1.10(c) of the Major League Baseball rule book read that "a bat may not be covered by such a substance more than 18 inches [46 cm] from the tip of the handle." At the time, such a hit was defined in the rules as "an illegally batted ball," and under the terms of the then-existing provisions of Rule 6.06, any batter who hit an illegally batted ball was automatically called out. The umpires concluded that under this interpretation, Brett's home run was disallowed, and he was out, thus ending the game.

MacPhail in his decision explained, however, that the "spirit of the restriction" about pine tar on bats was based not on the fear of unfair advantage, but simple economics; any contact with pine tar would discolor the ball, render it unsuitable for play, and require that it be discarded and replaced — thus increasing the home team's cost of supplying balls for a given game. In essence, MacPhail ruled that Brett had not violated the spirit of the rules, nor deliberately "altered [the bat] to improve the distance factor."

MacPhail's ruling was not without precedent. The umpires had previously come to a different conclusion in a 1975 game in which the Royals played the California Angels. The umpiring crew there did not negate one of John Mayberry's home runs for pine tar use. Deciding the protest, MacPhail upheld the umpires' decision with the same rationale, that the rule was established to prevent baseballs from being discolored during game play and that any discoloration to a ball leaving the ballpark did not affect the competitive balance.

MacPhail thus restored Brett's home run and ordered the game resumed with two outs in the top of the ninth inning with the Royals leading 5-4. Although MacPhail ruled that Brett's home run counted, he retroactively ejected Brett for the angry display against the umpire. He also ejected manager Dick Howser and coach Rocky Colavito for arguing with the umpires. Royals pitcher Gaylord Perry was ejected for giving the bat to the bat boy so he could hide it in the clubhouse. After delays and appeals the game finally resumed on August 18, a day off for both clubs, before a paltry 1,200 fans in Yankee Stadium. The Royals came to bat with two outs in the ninth and Hal McRae was retired. Dan Quisenberry retired the Yankees 1-2-3 in the bottom of the ninth, sealing the Royals victory.

One comment on the development of baseball doctrine: in 2010, Major League Baseball amended the official rules with a comment clarifying the consequences of using excessive pine tar on a bat. The comment codifies the interpretation of the MacPhail decision. The rule now states, "If no objections are raised prior to a bat's use, then a violation of Rule 1.10(c) on that play does not nullify any action or play on the field and no protests of such play shall be allowed."

George Brett's pine tar bat now resides in the Hall of Fame in Cooperstown, a testament to baseball's rules and the correct imposition of justice.

The moral of the story is that the literal and strict interpretation of the law or rule is not in itself sufficient to render a just decision.

In the spiritual realm, the intent of a rule and its effect on human souls in the moral order are always paramount. Here we see the doctrinal approach, which leads to a decision on the basis of what is written, and pastoral approach, which looks at intent of the rule and the greater good of the individual and community. These are classic Catholic principles rarely understood by the faithful. It has nothing to do with situational ethics the bankrupt view that wrong and right depend on the situation. This view leads to moral relativism where the majority rules or might makes right. This view is completely contrary to Catholic teaching. Let's examine more cases.

Consider two more type of infractions and see what baseball teaches about objective truth and the role of conscience. Jimmy Piersall was playing center field for the Indians against the Boston Red Sox when Ted Williams came to the plate. Piersall began jumping and dancing in center field in a deliberate effort to distract the batter. For this rule infraction he was ejected (for the sixth time that season).

A few years later, on June 23, 1963, the same Jimmy Piersall hit his hundredth career home run against the Phillies' Dallas Green at the Polo Grounds in New York. He decided to celebrate in an unusual fashion. Taking a few steps toward first he then turned around and ran the bases backward. In proper order, but backwards. Piersall did not violate the rules per se, but his lack of decorum created a bad example. The clowning center fielder immediately incurred the wrath of his tradition-loving manager and baseball sage Casey Stengel. Stengel cut Piersall soon after his novel home run jaunt.

In the first Piersall incident, the rule on the books prohibiting distraction of the batter is objectively clear. In other words, the rule applies to all players in all games. The decision-making that led Jimmy to behave in that manner is the subjective part. We don't know what he was thinking and if he thought his actions were correct. In this case, the rule strictly applies (like an objective truth); the player cannot by any means determine he knows better and violate the rule. Piersall incurred the penalty for his transgression — ejection from the game.

It is worth noting that not only did this impact Piersall personally, but his team suffered by losing a player upon which it was depending. Piersall failed to align his conscience with an objective truth (baseball rule) and behave in a manner expected of a pro ballplayer.

In the case of the backward home run jaunt, we see an infraction of unwritten rules that are part and parcel of the game. While these prohibitions do not have the weight and importance of the statutes in the official book of rules, nevertheless, they have an indispensable place in keeping good order. Here Piersall made a bad decision and suffered the consequence of his manager's displeasure.

Such a transgression merited another opportunity at

redemption, a chance to resume his career. Indeed, Piersall was granted that with — of all teams — the Angels! I guess he became angelic from that point on, as he finished his career playing four more years with the team before moving into the Angels' front office.

One more famous case of rule violation merits mention. On August 3, 1987, Joe Niekro was on the mound for the Twins, pitching against the Angels (somehow the Angels usually show up in these matters). The score was tied 2-2. Suddenly, the umpire noticed unusual movement on Niekro's knuckleball. The umpires converged on the mound to inspect Niekro for altering the baseball. Niekro was caught ditching both an emery board and a piece of sandpaper he had in his pocket. The pitcher was promptly ejected from the game and suspended for ten days. He missed a good part of a season in which his club would win the World Series. Niekro never exhibited any regret or even compunction for his transgressions. An example of a malformed conscience?

Imagine for a second that many or most Major League players did not know the rules and fine points of the game. Even more, suppose that most knew the rules pretty well but decided to pick and choose which rules they would follow. Now you have backward base running, treated bats, altered balls, illegal gloves, landscaping mischief, changing field dimensions, adding outs, cutting innings, and umpires conferring with fans to make decisions. This is a world where there is no objective truth. Everybody makes their own rules and most go along to get along. What would happen to baseball? Excellence would be gone, injury commonplace, records meaningless, fan support would dissipate, baseball's economy would crash, and on and on. Taken to its logical end, all that we love, appreciate, and revere about baseball would be lost.

Well, apply this analogy to any endeavor in life where there is no objective truth. The result in science would be to negate any objective manner of measurement. The physics formula $f = ma$ could be not-so-safely ignored — no consequences here at all! Mechanics would feel free to put water in your gas tank. Traffic signs might be seen as oppressive measures of the patriarchy that should best be ignored. Electricity can't be seen or touched; therefore, who needs codes and compliance? Medicine renounces its belief in male and female. It is all personal choice. Whether a child in the womb is alive or dead — or destined to be one way or another becomes a matter of choice. No one can say for sure that a beating heart is a sign of life despite the pulse being the first indication of a victim's condition. You get the picture. Ignoring objective truth and standards will result in chaos, bitterness, regret, and unhappiness.

We have seen one of the most extreme manifestations of relativism in the Nazi Holocaust, where the sacredness of innocent human life was denied and millions upon millions summarily sacrificed on the altar of choice. A tyrannical and maniacal government used its unmitigated power to choose who lived and who died.

Or how about we just arrive at decisions by consensus? Appeal to an "authority" who supports our position. Believe it or not, such was the case in the formative years of baseball. An 1876 rule stipulated that an umpire might confer with whomever he pleased, if he had been unable to see a play. This was a time when there was one umpire, but the practice was fraught with peril, as one can imagine. The rule was overturned in 1882. Rule 9.04(c) now bans umpires from conferring with players or fans in the crowd. Baseball has much to teach the culture in applying objective standards.

Fortunately, Major League Baseball has a long-standing, comprehensive, and coherent rules, rooted in tradition and experience that forever preserves the game's integrity. Should the baseball powers that be slip off into radical experimentation, disrupt the constants, or alter the delicate structural balance, it might very well lead to the sport's demise — no exaggeration.

From the diamond to the Vatican, the same principles apply. Found in Catholic teaching is the fullness of truth in faith and morals. This means that Christ established his Church, his body. Christ referred to himself as the Way, the Truth, and the Life. The

Catholic has access to the greatest system of morality ever revealed. Let's take these lessons from baseball's rules and their application in game situations and see what we can learn about the "Major League theology" found exclusively in the Catholic Church.

The first question is where do the rules in the Church come from? How is it possible for the Church to claim that it alone has the fullness of Faith and Truth?

The simple answer is Jesus Christ established the one, holy, catholic, and apostolic Church. All Catholics should be able to explain the four marks of the true Church. If you can't, you are not serious about the ball game or your life as a Christian. Furthermore Christ, who is the consummate team player, speaks and teaches very clearly through his Church. Recall that Christ never wrote a book and never told his followers to write a book. He chose twelve apostles and gave them power to forgive sins and change bread and wine into his Body and Blood. He told them to spread the Gospel teaching to all nations, baptizing them in the name of the Father, Son, and Holy Spirit.

The apostles received the fullness of the faith from Christ. Furthermore, Jesus told them of the coming of the Holy Spirit, who would guide them into "all truth," a clearer and clearer realization of the truth revealed in Christ. The apostles passed on Jesus' teaching, his deposit of truth, to their successors. This teaching authority is called the Church's Magisterium. It flows from Sacred Tradition which is the revelation that Jesus handed on to his apostles. It is this Tradition and the Magisterium that guided the Church during the first three centuries, before the New Testament was compiled and ratified.

Thus the Church came first, and gave us the Scriptures, not the other way around. In fact, it is Paul who tells us that the Church (the Catholic Church was the only one that existed at the time) is the foundation of truth. Paul tells Timothy, "I hope to come to you soon, but I am writing these instructions to you so that, if I am delayed, you may know how one ought to behave in the household of God, which is the Church of the living God, the pillar and bulwark of the truth" (1 Tm 3:14–15).

Paul also made the case for the role of natural law in an individual's search for the truth and moral rectitude. When writing to the Romans on a pressing moral issue, Paul states:

> For the wrath of God is revealed from heaven against all ungodliness and wickedness of men who by their wickedness suppress the truth. For what can be known about God is plain to them, because God has shown it to them. Ever since the creation of the world his invisible nature, namely, his eternal power and deity, can be clearly perceived in the things that have been made. So they are without excuse" (Romans 1:18–20).

God created every person in his image. Thus he placed the divine spark in each heart so that everyone can see the design of God inscribed in all creation and come to know the truth in the matter of "rules," which is to say, morality.

Finally, Christ provided for the visible head of the Church by appointing Peter first pope, who has been followed in an unbroken chain to our time with Francis, the 266th pope. Scripture, sacred Tradition, and the Magisterium are the tripod on which the authority of Christ is built. All guided by the Holy Spirit, according to the plan of the Father, with Jesus as head of his body. Thus the *Catechism* states clearly, "The Second Vatican Council's Decree on Ecumenism explains: 'For it is through Christ's Catholic Church alone, which is the universal help toward salvation, that the fullness of the means of salvation can be obtained'" (816). The Catholic Church alone possesses the fullness of truth in faith and orals.

Now, just as the Major League ballplayer is confronted with the challenge of being the best in terms of skill and execution, often in difficult circumstances, so, too, is the committed Catholic as a passionate follower of Christ. We need only look to the passages in the Gospel which support the teaching of two millennia. First, Christ tells us in John's Gospel, "If you love me, you will keep my commandments" (Jn 14:15). That means *all* the commandments. Earlier Christ set down the consequences in black and white regarding how we are to guide others. Jesus said to his disciples, "Temptations to sin are sure to come; but woe to him by whom they come! It would be better for him if a millstone were hung round his neck and he were cast into the sea, than that he should cause one of these little ones to sin" (Lk 17:1–2). Divine love is very clear on the embarrassment sin has caused the human race. Jesus Christ came precisely to raise our standard of play, to give us Major League moral aspirations, to show us the way to do what is supernatural instead of what is natural.

Let us now apply the three principles to the life of faith we noted earlier in the baseball rule situations.

First, a wrong call does not invalidate the rules. Jean Segura should have been out three times and yet he was not. But backward base running is still proscribed. Too often immorality or rule breaking is justified by, "He did it and nothing happened to him." Then there is the teenage mantra, "Everyone is doing it." Or how about polls in our day and age: XX% (pick your number) of Catholics don't not agree with the Church teaching on artificial contraception, abortion, homosexual activity, fornication, or adultery, as if polls carry any weight in the Gospel mandate of love. Jesus told the woman caught in adultery her sin is forgiven, yes, but then added, go and sin no more. As Archbishop Sheen explained in his writings, right is right if nobody is right and wrong is wrong if everybody is wrong.

Christ gave us the very best of examples. Jesus is the perfection of all virtues in his humanity and it is his example alone that we should look to measure the level or performance. Our neighbor — be they a priest, bishop, spouse, boss, or celebrity — is not the standard by which to measure our conduct. Christ alone is our model and guide. Moreover, he loves us too much to give us anything less than the best. How did he prove his love for us? By becoming man and living a humble, poor, obedient, and chaste life. He did that for us, not for his benefit. He took on flesh to suffer and die and reverse the effects of sin. Our Lord does not want us running the moral bases in reverse order. He never condones making our own rules, nor invalidating those that God has established.

So, if you disagree that the highest level of play is found in Christ's Church and its rule book, look again closely. Here are examples of serious sin that lead to eternal damnation;

- Failure to pray and orient our lives to God first; laziness in spiritual matters.
- Swearing in God's name.
- Missing Mass on Sundays and holy days of obligation.
- Neglect of parents and disregard for authority.
- Failure to instruct children in the Faith.
- Revenge, self-abuse through drugs and alcohol, contraception, abortion, euthanasia, suicide.
- Any sexual pleasure outside of married conjugal relations, including masturbation, fornication, adultery, sodomy.
- Lying, cheating, and stealing in serious matters.
- Bearing false witness or destroying another's good name, slander, and rash judgment.
- Envy, anger, and lust in thought, word, or deed.

These are Major League demands for sure. They should all be seen not so much as "breaking a rule" as a failure to love.

By "love" we mean the Gospel definition. At the heart of the Gospel definition of love is the cross. Jesus tells us to take up our cross and follow him daily, and this is not merely a metaphor. For following the Gospel requires sacrifice and hardship, the kind Major Leaguers invest to become the best.

Second, the pine tar game is a shining example of the correct application of the letter and spirit of the law. Here, Phil MacPhail restored Brett's home run while not excusing his behavior, upholding the ejection for his altercation with the umpire. Baseball's rules, like the Ten Commandments, are not established to punish, demean, or cause confusion. Hard, ironclad, unrelenting application of the law is slavery and abuse. Justice tempered with mercy demands that human considerations be taken into account — not to condone bad behavior, but to lift a person to true freedom and reach their divinely ordained potential.

This is at the heart of the running battle Jesus had with the Pharisees. They were more concerned about their authority and appearances than their impact on their neighbors. Jesus condemned the Pharisees, and while upholding every little part of the law, bade sinners to come to him. The Church is a hospital for sinners and not an elite club for saints or the successful. So great is the mercy of God that he can't resist us and longs to give us his forgiveness. That is why we have the sacrament of confession. In fact, according to Our Lord, the repentance of a sinner causes a party to be thrown in heaven. Jesus says, "I tell you, there will be more joy in heaven over one sinner who repents than over ninety-nine righteous persons who need no repentance" (Lk 15:7).

Third, let's examine the role of conscience. Recall that Piersall and Niekro were swiftly ejected from games in which they violated the rules. Piersall may not have known his dancing in the outfield would have resulted in his ejection, or he may have known and did not care; or maybe he knew and thought he should do it anyway to help the team. Niekro knew all along he was cheating. No matter the interior motivation, the consequence was the same. In these cases, the sanction happened to be immediate, but in life that is not always the case. So how does the role of conscience fit in our everyday decision-making at the plate?

Catholic Major League teaching on this is very clear. The first principle is one must never violate one's own conscience. One is never permitted to do what one's conviction says is wrong. Conscientious objectors are a prime example of this, as many have refused to take up arms for an unjust cause. Read the story of the

Nazi execution of Franz Jägerstätter to comprehend this basic and immutable rule of conscience. He was a simple Austrian husband and father who refused to serve in the Nazi army. For this he was hanged. His obedience to conscience stands as a rebuke to all those who went along with the Nazi war machine.

Second, our conscience must be properly formed. Simply, God is who we must please, because the purpose of our life is to know, love, and serve God, and be happy with him in eternity. In order for us to know how to fulfill our purpose our conscience must be formed by God's law and truth.

As Pope Saint John Paul II wrote in his encyclical *Veritatis Splendor*, conscience does not create the truth, conscience detects the truth. Our role on God's team is to know the rules, conform to them, and not be ejected from the game or the team. Appealing to conscience as a means of justifying clearly sinful behavior will not save one's soul. Furthermore, the damage inflicted on others or self may have lifetime consequences. As an example, a Catholic legislator votes for liberal abortion laws resulting in the state-approved death of children and harm to the mothers. No appeal to conscience can reverse this terrible tragedy. Recall the quote from Jerome Lejeune, "Only God truly forgives, man sometimes forgives, nature never forgives." God will forgive the repentant participant in the abortion, provided there is confession of sin to a priest; human relationships and lives may be irrevocably scarred; but the child can never be brought back to life.

Here is another thought on the beauty of Catholic teaching on justice and mercy in the Piersall case. Jimmy had severe mental health issues and even wrote a book, *Fear Strikes Out*, chronicling his battle with bipolar disorder. Suppose that, out of compassion, his antics were overlooked and even excused. The fights, distractions, arguments, and his helmet throwing were excused because of health reasons, or the "greater good of the team," or any number of reasons. Would that reflect love for the person, respect for the game, and care for the fans who pay to see a fair contest properly fought in the best spirit of competition? No, the sanctions and fines actually helped Jimmy become a productive ballplayer. Niekro, on the other hand, appeared on the David Letterman show discussing the cheating incident as if it were just business as usual. "Everybody does it" may be why everybody does not attain eternal happiness. Horrible thought!

Too often, immoral and improper behavior is excused under the guise of compassion. To avoid confrontation or criticism, we avoid admonishing the sinner. Consider the example of John the Baptist who Herod beheaded at the request of his wife, Herodias, whom he took from his brother: John the Baptist told the King it was wrong to take his brother's wife. John was loving and compassionate, caring about the soul of Herod. For this he paid with his life; Major Leaguer and a cousin of Jesus he was.

One final observation on rule infractions: an ejection, a fine, or dismissal from the team is not just a private matter. Baseball, like any team endeavor, mirrors life by having cheats and miscreants in the family. We are all sinners and all have fallen short of the glory of God. Whether it's the Black Sox scandal in baseball's formative years, Joe Niekro's emery-board ball-doctoring malpractice, Sammy Sosa's crooked corked bat, the use of performance-enhancing drugs, or the Astros sign-stealing scheme, the damage is always suffered by the sport and the team. All cheating is corporate and all sins echo in eternity. In like manner, the Catholic (or any Christian) can look at the passion of Jesus and see the effects of our sins on the Body of Christ first, and then on the Church, which is the mystical Body of Christ.

How many times have we heard the sophism, What I do in my bedroom is a private matter? No, it's not! Just look at our suffering Lord and see the damage our sins have wrought: the scourged and lacerated flesh of Jesus ripped to shreds because of sexual impurity; the crown of thorns slammed on his sacred head to atone for the sins of pride; the gouge in his shoulder from the beam of the cross, carried to overcome personal spiritual sloth; the parched lips and severe thirst resulting from gluttony, gossip, slander, and filthy language; the nails holding his hands to the wood because of avarice, greed, and theft; the pinioned feet fastened there by personal anger or revenge; and the mockery of the spectators endured for the sins of vanity. Our sins did all of that!

Yet, in the end a soldier opens Our Lord's Sacred Heart and Saint John testifies that blood and water flowed out. The Church Father's teach us that the way to divine love is opened with a spear. Blood and water flowed out immediately, the water representing the regeneration of souls in baptism (the Major League Catholic uniform); the blood portending the Eucharist and remission of sin through his sacrifice on the cross. Our Lord suffered to save us from our sins. At the cross and through his blood there is forgiveness and mercy. At the altar during Mass the very same sacrifice is offered and our souls are nourished by that same flesh and blood from Calvary in the Eucharist.

A final point in closing this meditation. The Ten Commandments, natural law, and objective truth are under relentless attack in our culture, and, in fact, around the world. Catholic teaching on faith and morals, especially on sexuality, is mocked, rejected, ridiculed, misrepresented, ignored, and maligned — identical to how the Lord was treated during his passion. For perseverance and strength, we turn to the words of Paul, "But even if we, or an angel from heaven, should preach to you a gospel contrary to that which we preached to you, let him be accursed" (Gal 1:8). Moreover, Paul tells Timothy, "Do not be ashamed then of testifying to our Lord ... but take your share of suffering for the gospel" (2 Tm 1:8). A Major Leaguer does not leave his skills and knowledge at the high school, college, or minor league level. It's the same in your spiritual life with prayer, study, and good works. You shouldn't be an eighth-grade confirmation Catholic forever. Be the Major Leaguer Christ called you to be — a faithful, committed Catholic.

After considering all this, I offer a prayer:

Father, grant me the grace of turning away from sin and becoming one with Christ your Son in the Sacraments of Penance and the Holy Eucharist obtained for me at such great price. God, grant me the grace also to see my sins as the cause of Christ's horrific suffering: to understand that sin is not just breaking the rules, but is really hurting the ones I love. Give me the strength to love by answering my Savior's plea, "If you love me, you will keep my commandments." Amen.

QUESTIONS FOR REFLECTION – THE INTENTIONAL WALK

BALL ONE

Can I explain how God's laws and commandments prove his love for me and our love for others? Out of love, do I strive to lead teammates on the base paths of holiness offering care, support, and prayer to save them from sinful choices, no matter the cost to me?

BALL TWO

When recognizing the sin in my life, do I see it as a failure to love? Can I suppress my pride and accept Church teaching on faith and morals as coming from Christ?

BALL THREE

Are God's laws meant to free us? How? Do I see the commandments and Church teaching on faith and morals as coming directly from Christ? From my Lord who wishes for my joy to be complete in this life and the life to come?

BALL FOUR

Do I review nightly how I have or have not loved God today? If not, am I willing to begin a daily examination of conscience?

—ON DECK—

Saint John Bosco *(HOF)*

"Enjoy yourself as much as you like — if only you keep from sin. Health is God's great gift and we must spend it entirely for him. Our eyes should see only for God, our feet walk only for him, our hands labor for him alone; in short, our entire body should serve God while we still have time."

9TH INNING

Election to the Hall of Fame (HOF) – Death, Judgment, Heaven, Hell (DJHH)

So teach us to number our days that we may get a heart of wisdom.
— Psalm 90:12

Baseball's Hall of Fame opened in Cooperstown in 1939. Among the first inductees was Albert G. Spalding of pitching and sporting goods company fame. He was the principal architect behind the Mills Commission, which promulgated the story of baseball's founding in Cooperstown by Abner Doubleday. Part of the inaugural festivities was a baseball game played by some of the newly enshrined Hall of Famers against some future Hall of Famers on the field where Doubleday supposedly organized the first game. Doubleday Field remains, but, paradoxically, Abner Doubleday is not in the Hall of Fame! There are eternal lessons to learn from who made it to the Hall and who did not.

Cooperstown is baseball's ultimate honor — one only bestowed on the game's greats. It celebrates those who succeed spectacularly in a game of failure; and sometimes those who fail spectacularly in their success. Let's consider three stories of baseball greats to illustrate some great spiritual truths.

Pete Rose is not in the Hall of Fame — a player, who one can argue, God made for Major League Baseball. Charlie Hustle, a moniker that aptly describes his style of play, is the all-time Major League leader in hits (4,256); games played (3,562); at bats (14,053); and singles (3215). Furthermore, Rose won three batting titles, two Gold Gloves, three World Series, one MVP Award, and Rookie of the Year. Remarkably, he made All Star appearances at five different positions and once had a 44-game hitting streak, the third longest in Major League Baseball history. Certainly, an illustrious 24-year career of virtually unparralleled accomplishment. Yet the door to his baseball canonization remains barred.

I had the great pleasure to meet Pete at the MGM Grand in Las Vegas early in 2020 when I attended an industry trade show. I was walking to my room when I passed Pete signing autographs for those who bought expensive memorabilia. I purchased a copy of a *Sports Illustrated* cover that featured Pete's admission of gambling. He signed my *SI* cover copy, and we spoke briefly. I mentioned how much I admired his play when I was a young teenager and tried to emulate his hustle and intensity. (Pete's influence stayed with me through adulthood; embarrassingly, I was ejected from a slow-pitch softball game for colliding with the shortstop at second base to break up a double play). I still vividly remember Pete's 1970 All Star-game-ending-collision with catcher Ray Fosse.

We spoke of some of the great pitchers Pete faced, and he knew his batting average against all of them. I explained that I was a lifelong Phillies fan who hated him when he played for the Reds, but was so excited when he became a Phil. I explained that his catch of the foul ball off Bob Boone's glove in the 1980 World Series was classic Rose. Finally, I asked Pete if he thought he would be admitted to the Hall. Pete said curtly, "Naw, I'm over it." I really don't think Pete is over it.

Rose's problem was gambling; specifically, Rose bet on baseball, even games in which he was involved. For that sole reason he was banned from the game. The Hall of Fame ruled that a banned person cannot stand for election. So Pete Rose remains, perhaps forever, at the threshold. It's a tragedy that a life of dedication, work, hustle, and accomplishment built on God-given talent and drive cannot be accorded baseball's ultimate honor.

Juan Marichal is in the Hall of Fame, but like Rose, he may not have been if not for his "time in purgatory," so to speak, and the humble way he handled the delay.

Marichal had a stellar pitching career with the San Francisco Giants. His debut against the Phillies on July 19, 1960, was a masterful complete game shutout in which he faced only 29 batters. Between that game and retirement on April 16, 1975, Juan won 243 games versus a loss record of 142. His career ERA was a stellar 2.89 with 52 shutouts and 10 All Star appearances.

He also pitched in one of the greatest duels of all time. On July 2, 1963, Marichal faced off with fellow Hall of Famer Warren Spahn. With five future Hall of Famers in the batting ranks (the Giants' Willie Mays, Willie McCovey, and Orlando Cepeda, and the Braves' Henry Aaron and Eddie Mathews), Spahn and Marichal still threw fifteen shutout innings, tossing over 200 pitches each. The gem of a game at Candlestick Park in San Francisco finally ended in the bottom of the sixteenth, after midnight, when Mays launched a Spahn screwball into the left-field stands for a home run.

With pitching like that and his overall record, Juan should have been in the Hall of Fame on the first ballot. He was not elected on that occasion; nor on the second ballot bearing his name.

The impediment on the road to Cooperstown for Juan was an ugly incident with Dodger catcher John Roseboro that tainted his lofty lifetime accomplishments. In the heat of the pennant race in August 1965, the Dodgers came to Candlestick Park with Marichal facing the Dodgers and Sandy Koufax. Each pitcher in the early innings had knocked down hitters and the umpire warned each against further retaliation.

Marichal came to bat in the third inning. After Koufax's second pitch, Roseboro's return throw to his pitcher either grazed Marichal's ear or came close enough to trigger a reaction. Marichal turned and hit Roseboro twice with his bat opening up a two-inch gash on the catcher's head that required fourteen stitches. A bench-clearing brawl erupted. Marichal was ejected from the game, suspended for another eight games (two starts) and fined a then-record $1,750 (a penalty many baseball pundits and fans considered lenient). Roseboro filed a suit for damages that was later settled out of court. But the damage to Marichal's reputation could not be resolved that quickly. It would linger for years, eventually manifesting itself in the Hall of Fame snubs.

With the road to Cooperstown and pitching immortality seemingly blocked, Divine Providence intervened. Ironically, Marichal had ended his career with the Dodgers and was consequently invited back to Dodger Stadium in 1982 for an old-timer's game. Roseboro was also there. The two men became friends. In a subsequent telephone call, Marichal asked Roseboro to forgive him. Roseboro responded by publicly appearing with Marichal, even playing in his charity golf tournament in the Dominican Republic. After the display of mutual public forgiveness, Marichal was elected to the Hall of Fame on the very next ballot. Released from purgatory he joined baseballs immortals.

Then there is the saga of Bill Mazeroski. On October 13, 1960, in the seventh game of the World Series, the Pirate led off the ninth inning at Forbes Field. Not only was the series tied at 3-3, but the game was tied 9-9. The first pitch from Yankee hurler Bill Terry was a ball. Mazeroski connected on the second pitch and sent it sailing over the head of left fielder Yogi Berra and the ivy-covered brick wall for a home run, the first and only time a seventh game of the World Series was decided by a home run.

In an instant Mazeroski's life changed. He would never tire of speaking or hearing about that iconic moment that would propel him into the Hall of Fame. But that took time.

Mazeroski played all his seventeen seasons with the Pirates. Maz, as he was called, sported a respectable (at least for a second baseman) lifetime batting average of .260. He did not put up dominating stats like Pete Rose or Juan Marichal. What Maz did was quietly go about the business of playing defense. And it was defense like no one else ever played. Day to day, game to game he dug out ground balls in the infield dirt and turned double plays like nobody else. He was even part of two triple plays in his career. So proficient was he at his craft that announcer Bob Prince called him "the glove." He earned eight Gold Glove awards, had a career .983 fielding percentage, led the National League in assists nine times, and holds the MLB record for double plays by a second baseman. In Bill James' *Historical Baseball Abstract*, he writes, "Bill Mazeroski's defensive statistics are probably the most impressive of any player at any position." Statistically, no other player comes as close to fielding perfection as Maz.

He retired in 1972. Underappreciated, it would be almost thirty years before he would be judged fit to enter Cooperstown. One glorious moment amidst a career of toil and routine plays –and dazzling ones that no doubt won bunches of games for the Pirates— and Maz finally made it to the Hall.

We've seen three different paths to Major League glory, but only two of our players were elected to the Hall of Fame, with one banished forever. All three men had long careers by baseball standards, but like all worldly things they seem to have passed so quickly, in retrospect.

So what are the Major League Catholic lessons for us? It is simply what the Church and Scriptures teach: life is fleeting (as the psalmist says, our lives pass "like foam on the water") while eternity is forever. When the record book closes on our earthly existence only four things remain: death, judgment, heaven, hell.

Let the wise man beware. Let him learn from these three illustrious baseball brothers three Major League Catholic truths. First, just one unforgiven and unrepented mortal sin will condemn a soul to hell for all eternity. Second, God is love; in his mercy he knows we need forgiveness, just as we need to forgive others. Third, it is the utmost folly not to prepare for death. Let's draw the parallels.

Pete Rose will never be in the Hall for the transgression of gambling and betting on his own team. We see similar fates in Scripture. Lucifer, the most glorious of all created angels, rebelled against God one catastrophic time and for that singular sin was cast into hell for eternity. Similarly, our first parents, Adam and

Eve, disobeyed and were banished from paradise for a single act of disobedience against divine love. Moses did not enter the Promised Land for his single moment of doubt and anger. David lost the unity of his kingdom because of his single act of adultery with Bathsheba. These examples should sear into our hearts the monstrous enormity of sin and how much pain it caused our blessed Lord during his crucifixion and death. What should result is a firm resolve to never commit serious sin. It is worse than death because its consequence is eternal rejection of God and an eternity of unspeakable suffering. Note that Jesus, in the Gospel, speaks ten more times of hell than he does of heaven. Hell is real. Pete Rose's baseball fate on earth should not be the Catholic's in eternity. Our firm resolution should be to confess all serious sin to a priest in the confessional, with a firm resolve not to sin again.

Now, if one confesses serious sin, than the mercy of God knows no bounds. The Father has prepared a place for his children in heaven, and it is gained by fervent sorrow, confession of sin, and repentance. Love, then, is the primary reason to be sorry for sin: because of how much sin hurts Our Lord. This is perfect contrition. Moreover, serious sin deprives the soul of grace and ruptures our relationship with God. Fear of hell is another reason for sorrow for sin (this is called "imperfect contrition," but sacramental absolution grants us forgiveness for these offenses). Let us grow so much in love with Jesus that love casts out fear, and love becomes the sole reason for our sorrow and resolve to sin no more.

Now a portrait of mercy. Juan Marichal and John Roseboro offer a beautiful story of reconciliation. In this case, forgiveness flowered into a friendship that continued throughout the rest of their lives. When Roseboro passed away, Marichal was an honorary pall bearer. He even said he wished he had John as his catcher. Sandy Koufax said to Marichal that he would have loved to have John as his catcher. Thus the triumphant of the goodness of grace freed Marichal from the ongoing consequences of the horrible scene that took place in 1965. There is Major League Catholic theology in play here, for eternal salvation depends on forgiveness and reconciliation. Jesus instructs us, "So if you are offering your gift at the altar and remember that your brother has something against you, leave your gift there before the altar and go; first be reconciled to your brother and then come and offer your gift" (Mt 5:23–24).

Even more sobering is the stunning reciprocity to which we commit ourselves in the Lord's Prayer: "Forgive us our trespasses as we forgive those who trespass against us." Stop and consider those words Our Lord gave us from his own lips. We ask the Father to forgive us in the same way we forgive others. Failure to forgive others is tantamount to self-condemnation.

In Scripture we see two of heaven's Hall of Famers experience of forgiveness — one offering Christ's forgiveness to others and one receiving that forgiveness. The Book of Acts recounts the stoning of Stephen, the first Christian martyr. "And as they were stoning Stephen, he prayed, 'Lord Jesus, receive my spirit.' And he knelt down and cried with a loud voice, 'Lord, do not hold this sin against them'" (Acts 7:59–60). This was a truly Christlike act of extending forgiveness, and the heavens opened to Stephen's vision in response.

One by-stander, who was watching over the cloaks of the murderers, was a zealot named Saul. He colluded in this heinous act. A short time later, while on a mission to round up other Christians to suffer Stephen's fate, Saul met Jesus on the road to Damascus. Once he met Christ, Saul's life was radically changed. He would become better known to us as the apostle Paul. Forgiveness transformed Paul into the very image of Christ as he suffered so much for the Gospel.

Of course, we have the example of Jesus with the first words from the cross, "Father, forgive them; for they know not what they do" (Lk 23:34).

Catholics should take heed and resolve to love in this sacrificial manner. Like Juan entering the Hall, a time in purgatory may be our ticket to heaven. Yes, purgatory. Read and study this love-inspired doctrine of the Catholic Faith if you want to understand the deeper game. Work to acquire a Major League understanding of the

Faith and not languish at a level of T-ball theology.

Now we come to the Catholic lessons learned at second base through Maz. His one at bat won a World Championship amidst an otherwise pedestrian career, even if he did play stellar defense. Here we see the need to be ready for that one opportunity that life may offer: a game-ending, series-ending, perhaps life-ending blast at glory and fame. Mazeroski capitalized on his one shot, but he worked hard day after day to be in a position to hit that magic home run.

Such is sometimes the case with holy souls who become saints! Here are a few examples. St. Thomas More had such a glorious moment when he was beheaded in sixteenth-century England by a king who would not obey the marriage laws of the Church. St Maria Goretti was murdered by a neighboring Italian youth because she would not submit to his impure advances. St. Maximilian Kolbe, a Polish Franciscan priest, gave his life for a married prisoner, taking his place in the starvation bunker at the Auschwitz concentration camp. These three Hall of Famers were ready for the moment of death, really the moment of glory, as we all should be. For that is a moment none can escape, and it is sheer folly not to meditate on this moment frequently. Not morbidly, but with joy, because for the Catholic striving for perfection death is the culmination of exchanging our life for Christ's. We give Christ our mortality and he gives us his divinity. Like a game-winning home run in the World Series, a single instant can change the trajectory of our destiny. It is essential that we play hard, day in and day out, to be prepared for that big moment.

Here is a parallel story in Scripture, the most exciting play in the Bible. Usually, fans will say that two of the rarest and most exciting plays in baseball are the triple play and stealing home. Stealing home is almost a lost art. Ty Cobb holds the record with 54 steals of home. It is rarely attempted now since pitchers have learned to use the stretch position with runners on third. But it can happen. It's most successful when a runner sees an unusual situation and seizes the moment. Maybe it succeeds precisely because it's so unexpected. Imagine stealing home to win a World Series game. Or how about stealing home with the game tied, in the bottom of the ninth, in the seventh game of the World Series? That would be a highlight film for the ages.

Scripture gives us just such a highlight play for the ages. It happened on Calvary. Our Lord hung on the cross between two thieves, traditionally known as Dismas and Gestas. Gestas blasphemed: If you are the Son of God, save yourself, save us! Come down off that cross.

But, the other thief saw an enormous opportunity. At the moment of death, he made his move. He said, in essence: We deserve to die, but this man has done nothing wrong. Jesus, remember me when you come into your kingdom.

Jesus said to him: "Truly I say to you, today you will be with me in paradise" (Lk 23:43). Thus the good thief, in the bottom of the ninth, in the last moment of his life, *stole home!*

It might well be said that Dismas made a perfect act of contrition to our ultimate high priest, as Jesus is described in the New Testament's Book of Hebrews. He displayed *faith* in Jesus' mission as the Messiah (how else would he have foreseen Jesus coming into his kingdom, particularly at that moment), he had *hope* that Jesus would honor his request, and he exhibited *love* in defending Jesus against the other thief's mockery.

Mazeroski and Dismas, by crossing the plate those fateful afternoons, changed their destinies forever. Likewise, each of their "plays for the ages" catapulted both to their respective Hall of Fames.

One final point is worth pondering: Cooperstown glory will fade and ultimately disappear, as will all earthly things. But the crown of eternal glory won by Dismas will never perish. Remember always the four last things — death, judgment, heaven, hell — and prepare for that glorious moment when the Father calls you home. May our careers be such that we hear the words, "This day you will be with me in paradise."

Saint Paul exhorts the faithful, "Therefore, my beloved, as

you have always obeyed, so now, not only as in my presence but much more in my absence, work out your own salvation with fear and trembling; for God is at work in you, both to will and to work for his good pleasure" (Phil 2:12–13). We have one career — a short one at that. There is no second chance. Death and judgment await us all and often come "like a thief in the night."

One last word of encouragement. Pete Rose drove in 1,314 runs during his career. That stat is nowhere near Hank Aaron's all -time record of 2,297, but impressive enough to put Rose at 103rd on the all-time list. That number reflects continual effort and success over a great amount of time. But in the ballpark of Major League Catholic requirements it can be of no avail. As our blessed Lord states, "For what does it profit a man, to gain the whole world but forfeit his life?" (Mk 8:36). Imagine if Pete would employ his gifts of time, accomplishment, celebrity, and influence to drive just one runner into our heavenly home?

This is the good news that should encourage all of us to become apostles seeking to save others. In the New Testament we read:

> My brethren, if any one among you wanders from the truth and someone brings him back, let him know that whoever brings back a sinner from the error of his way will save his soul from death and will cover a multitude of sins. (James 5:19–20)

In other words, if you save one soul, bring a brother or sister back from a path of sin and error, you cover a multitude of past sins and, like Dismas, ready yourself to receive the Lord's gift of salvation.

May we all be safe at home!

— —

QUESTIONS FOR REFLECTION - THE INTENTIONAL WALK

BALL ONE

How have I used the gifts and talents that God has given me? Can I earnestly say I am striving for holiness — that is, to do God's will? Can I honestly say that my priorities are first God, then others, and myself last?

BALL TWO

Do I understand and contemplate that I will undergo the particular judgment at the moment of death and must render an account for my conduct, and that one unrepented serious sin can send me to eternal damnation?

BALL THREE

What am I doing at this moment concretely to prepare for death and judgment? Am I striving to grow in my faith, love Jesus more and more, and root out my sins and faults?

BALL FOUR

Do I pray daily for the dying, the sick, the souls in purgatory, and for my own happy death? Do I desire to die in the presence of Jesus and Mary?

—ON DECK—

Saint John of the Cross *(HOF)*

"It is great wisdom to know how to be silent and to look at neither remarks, nor the deeds, nor the lives of others. … In the evening of life we will be judged on love alone."

POST GAME WRAP UP - G.O.A.T.s

How could these reflections on baseball's Catholic parallels be complete without some thought as who was the G.O.A.T. — the Greatest of All Time to don a Major League uniform and the greatest to don the garment of grace in the kingdom of heaven.

This discussion is important for two widely divergent reasons. Baseball's greatest is food for thought and comparison, which leads to great fun (if sometimes heated) conversations. The debate deepens one's knowledge of the sport and may even lead to religious discussion (hint, after reading this work), but, admittedly, usually has no lasting impact on one's destiny. While the "greatest in the Kingdom" is quite the opposite: that Major Leaguer in the Kingdom of God is not only worthy of emulation, but this saint can very well help us to radically improve our game. In short, this great saint can be our friend, mentor and spiritual father. Let's name both our heroes who are noted for their power and impact — one on baseball and the other the Church.

Our selection for the greatest baseball player will come as no surprise. His impact on the game is undeniable, and he was superlative both on the mound and at the plate (extremely rare in the big leagues). Moreover, he was Catholic, educated in a religious school, and later a member of the Knights of Columbus. He was also noted for some non-virtuous activity, but he frequently displayed great kindness and charity. He was a larger-than-life figure who loved the attention and fame afforded him by his achievements, which far outstripped his contemporaries on the field. He changed the game in ways that endure to this day — such was his impact, using the talents and opportunity afforded him by our blessed Lord. By now you can guess that our pick for the G.O.A.T. is George Herman Ruth Jr.

Born in Baltimore, Maryland (some attribute the state's name to its Catholic population's honoring of the Blessed Mother), Ruth was introduced to baseball while attending St. Mary's Industrial School for boys, which was run by the Xaverian Brothers. Ruth credited the better part of his character formation to Brother Matthias, the school's disciplinarian and baseball lover. Ruth would later say that his playing style mirrored that of his first mentor. After he became famous, Ruth would visit St Mary's. He always supported the school through donations and appearing at fund-raisers. He even purchased cars for Brother Matthias.

Ruth first played pro ball in 1914 for the Baltimore minor league club. He was quickly sold that year to the Boston Red Sox, where he performed as a pitcher. He became the ace of the Red Sox's staff by 1916. The next year, he began making the switch to outfield while also pitching through 1918. In 1919, his prowess as a power hitter emerged just as baseball was entering the live ball era. But it was in 1920, after being traded to the Yankees, that he rocked the baseball world.

His performance that year was breathtaking. Ruth batted .376, hit 36 doubles, nine triples, scored 158 runs, batted in 137 runs, and accumulated a slugging percentage of .847. Ruth hit 54 homers while no other team total that year was more than 44!

The impact of Ruth's record-breaking year on the game was immediate. The sport was reeling from the Black Sox scandal — the deliberate tanking in the previous year's World Series at the direction of gamblers — but fans flocked to see Ruth hit his blasts. Players imitated his powerful upward swing and even copied the type of bat he used (a thinner handle for more speed). Batting averages went up around the leagues, as did scores (and strikeouts, by the way). The Babe started a trend in baseball that continues up to the present moment, with teams happily trading strike outs for more home runs, as most players swing for the fences.

By the time Ruth's twenty-two-year career ended, his achievements were glaringly disproportionate to his contemporaries.

Having hit 49 homers with Boston in six seasons, it was in 1921, his third year as a full-time player, that Ruth became the all-time career home run king. He would go on to break his own record 577 times. When he retired in 1935 with 714 homers, the second-place challenger was Lou Gehrig with a meager 378 round-trippers. Ruth's amazing stats include career totals for runs batted in (RBIs), 2,213; bases on balls, 2,062; slugging percentage, .690; and on base plus slugging percentage (OPS), 1.164. The last two stats remain all-time Major League records. In 1939, Ruth was elected into the Baseball Hall of Fame as one of its inaugural class members. He was a member of three World Series championship teams with Boston and four with the Yankees.

The Sultan of Swat (one of his widely known nicknames) was, as we've indicated, an accomplished pitcher. In his six seasons with Boston, he won 89 games and recorded a 2.19 ERA. He had a four-year stretch where he was second in the AL in wins and ERA behind the legendary Walter Johnson. (Ruth had a winning record against the Big Train in head-to-head matchups). In the 1918 World Series, against the Cubs, Ruth pitched 29 2/3 scoreless innings. This record stood until 1961 when it was broken by Yankee great Whitey Ford. Whitey pitched 14 innings for what remains the longest complete game victory in World Series history.

Notably, the Babe hit the first home run in Yankee Stadium history when the park opened in 1923. He also hit the first home run in All Star Game history in 1933 while playing for the Connie Mack-managed American League stars. His final two home runs were hit in Forbes Field against the Pirates while playing for the Boston Braves.

Our hero was not without major shortcomings. In many respects Ruth was not a model to emulate. His dietary indiscretions were legendary. The story goes that his gluttony was responsible for the pin stripes on Yankee uniforms. A heavyset Ruth retuning to spring practice motivated Yankee owner Jacob Ruppert to change the team's outfit, in hopes of hiding Ruth's girth. The Bambino fought with umpires and fans. Moreover, he was a notorious curfew breaker, if they even had curfews back then. Ruth reportedly could not remember his teammates' names. He spent his fortune liberally, sometimes foolishly, and often generously. And, to his credit, he was remorseful when reproved for his wayward behavior, and recommitted to the narrow path.

His background before St. Mary's likely played a role in his misbehavior. He was the son of a saloon keeper and his mother died when he was twelve, after which he was sent to a reform school as an incorrigible.

After fulfilling his unique role in the world, Ruth died of cancer on August 16, 1948 (one day after the feast of the Assumption). We pray that our heavenly Mother was there to greet him on that last trip to home — the only home run that really counted.

We close here with a quote from Ruth's teammate Harry Hooper: "Sometimes I still can't believe what I saw. This nineteen-year-old kid, crude, poorly educated, only lightly brushed by the social veneer we call civilization, gradually transformed into the idol of American youth and the symbol of baseball the world over — a man loved by more people and with an intensity of feeling that perhaps has never been equaled before or since."

Such is Divine Providence, and such is the extraordinary impact of the great game of baseball on an otherwise ordinary life.

So now we turn our attention to The Greatest in the Kingdom and his impact on the Church and our lives.

Like Ruth, he is a man of extraordinary power, given special graces and talents to fill a unique role in salvation. He, too, took a piece of wood in his hands to make a daily living. Furthermore, he, too, was a husband and father tasked with the sublime duties of providing for a family. And, like Ruth, his greatness, bestowed by God the Father, can be measured by the impact of his life on others.

Unlike Ruth, however, this man possessed the fullness of virtue. Instead of performing in the greatest city of world, The Greatest labored in obscurity, in a town considered the offscouring of the earth. Whereas Ruth acquired fame and fortune, our hero encountered rejection and poverty. While Ruth broke the rules and pushed the envelope, our saint was obedient to civil and religious authority, as an expression of his love for God. And, finally, unlike Ruth, who was a public figure, gave speeches, and was often quoted, The Greatest never wrote a word, made a public appearance or ever had a quote attributed to him. In fact, he had few possessions, no memorials from his contemporaries that we know of, and, incredibly, no grave marks his passing. We are not even sure when he died.

How can the baseball's immortal Ruth and The Greatest in the Kingdom be so dissimilar you ask? It may be rooted in another uncanny similarity between baseball and the Catholic Church — the paradox. Baseball, like Scripture, is full of paradoxes. For example, baseball is structured so that the defense has the ball; a batted ball that hits the foul pole is fair; foul territory is in play (in fact, the catcher plays almost the entire game in foul territory); stealing is a virtue; the catcher is credited with a putout on a pitcher's strikeout; new, clean baseballs are rubbed with mud; and the batter who sacrifices remains in the game.

Scripture (the Bible is the quintessential Catholic book) offers such divine wisdom, always turning the maxims of the world on their heads. For example, consider these inspired paradoxes: the first shall be last and the last shall be first; blessed are the poor; whoever saves his life will lose it, but whoever loses his life will save it; therefore I take pleasure in infirmities, in reproaches, in necessities, in persecutions, in distresses for Christ's sake: for when I am weak, then am I strong; and, one more, he who exalts himself will be humbled and he who humbles himself will be exalted.

By any measure, The Greatest in the Kingdom must be very different from the greatest on the ball field. In fact, our blessed Lord's words to James and John when they ask to sit on Jesus' right and left in the Kingdom contradicts any such ambition: "And whoever would be first among you must be your slave" (Mt 20:27). A life of service to others is the hallmark of Hall of Famers in the Kingdom.

So, then, who conformed his life to these radical teachings

and most closely resembles Christ? Who is the greatest in the Catholic Hall of Fame because of the impact he had on the Church and the world? **It is Saint Joseph!**

Saint Joseph is the foster father of Jesus, husband of Mary, descendant of King David, and the carpenter from Nazareth. He is the servant of all, working in anonymity, suffering greatly, protecting his newborn child, and providing for the Holy Family. He is the greatest because he placed God above all things ,and God the Father in turn entrusted to him his greatest possession — his divine Son. Thus, for each of us, Joseph is a model, a patron and most importantly *a father in the spiritual life!*

Let's contemplate briefly the greatness of Joseph under his seven patronages.

Saint Joseph is Protector of the Universal Church. Proclaimed by Pope Pius IX on December 8, 1870, the Church acknowledges the greatness of St. Joseph's dignity as the earthly father of Jesus. Joseph protected Baby Jesus in his human body from the wicked designs of Herod, who sought the life of the Child. As Joseph saved the Child Jesus from this corrupt government official, so does Joseph protect the mystical Body of Christ when it faces dangers from enemies. Joseph will continue to be a father and protector to the one, holy, catholic, and apostolic Church. Beseech him in times of distress in the Church.

Saint Joseph is the head of the Holy Family. He was obedient to God's will in taking Mary for his wife. Joseph found shelter in Bethlehem for the birth of his son. He also took the Child and his mother and fled to Egypt as the angel instructed.

Moreover, Joseph returned with his family to Nazareth where he provided for their needs by the work of his hands. Luke tells us that "and [Jesus] went down with them and came to Nazareth, and was obedient to them. ... And Jesus increased in wisdom and in stature, and in favor with God and man" (Lk 2:51–52). Joseph longs to help all families who have recourse to him, as did Mary and Jesus.

Saint Joseph is the Patron of Workers. He was a carpenter.

We know his trade from one Scripture verse about Jesus: "Is not this the carpenter's son?" (Mt 13:55). Consequently, Joseph is model for all workmen — for all who labor in offices, factories, fields, and the Church. Joseph's work was to care for his family and neighbor at the service of God. He also labored for souls, which is the only reason the Divine Child came to earth in his care. Joseph is always willing to help us in our temporal and spiritual labors.

Saint Joseph is the Comfort of the Sick. Many saints have credited the intercession of Joseph with a special cure in their lives. St. Joseph's Oratory in Montreal, founded by St. Andre Bessette, contains the crutches and canes of the afflicted who were helped by Andre through the intercession of Joseph. We, too, can ask for our holy patron's prayers in times of sickness and suffering.

Saint Joseph is the Patron of a Happy Death. There is no evidence that Joseph was present during Jesus public ministry; therefore, we can conclude that Joseph died in Nazareth. This was a most happy death, in the presence of Jesus and Mary, and the reason for him being known as the patron of a happy death. To die in the arms of Jesus and Mary should — no, must — be the most ardent desire of our souls. What better way to fulfill this desire that to have recourse to Joseph? Go to him now and remain in the state of grace through frequent confession of sin to a priest. Joseph will come to the aid of all God's spiritual children at the hour of death.

Saint Joseph is the Patron of Travelers. Scripture recalls for us the journey to Bethlehem at the time of the census so that the prophecy of Our Lord's birth could be fulfilled. As stated, the Holy Family then journeyed to Egypt and finally back to Nazareth. We also know that the Holy Family went to Jerusalem for the feasts, during which Jesus was left behind when he was twelve years old. Travel was done on foot, over rough terrain, in dangerous conditions. On our own journeys we can entrust our travels to the protection of Joseph. He will never leave our side, just as he was present every moment in service to Jesus and Mary.

Saint Joseph is the Terror of Demons. Jesus, known as

the son of the carpenter, came to earth to save mankind from the embarrassment of sin by crushing Satan's head on Golgotha (which means place of the skull). Because of Joseph's unique relationship to our blessed Lord and his cooperation in the work of salvation, Joseph is given a unique title: Terror of Demons. Furthermore, in his virginal relationship with Mary was pure of heart, and this quality alone causes the devils to flee. Joseph can help his children ward off attacks of lust and the many temptations to impurity so prevalent in today's culture. Joseph, who defended Jesus and Mary from so many evils, will also protect his spiritual sons and daughters in the same way. Have recourse to him.

One final difference between Babe Ruth and Saint Joseph: Ruth never made it into the coaching or managerial ranks of the sport he played so well. Conversely, Joseph, head of the family to whom God himself in Jesus was obedient, now sits beside his son in the Kingdom. He is, after all, head of the Household of God.

To join Saint Joseph's Household (or team), I encourage you to purchase a copy of the book *Consecration to St. Joseph: The Wonders of Our Spiritual Father* by Donald H. Calloway, MIC. In this work, baseball fans will learn so much about the Greatest in the Kingdom. Babe Ruth's achievements, monumental as they are, will appear in comparison as so much dust. In learning about Saint Joseph, you will come to understand that truly Major League spiritual life is found in the Catholic Church. You will find also the gifts, knowledge, coaching, grace, and support to become and remain holy men and women.

Consecrate yourself to St. Joseph. You will be happy to be on his ball club — now and in eternity.

Saint Joseph, pray for us
March 19, 2021
Feast of Saint Joseph
In the Year of Saint Joseph

ADDITIONAL SPIRITUAL RESOURCES

(Now that you've qualified for the Catholic World Series)

First, A Word of Gratitude to Mothers

Saint Joseph may be the G.O.A.T. of Catholic spirituality for men, but we'd be remiss if we did not express our gratitude to the Blessed Mother, as well as to our own mothers, who have sacrificed so much to give us ballplayers life.

Busy as she was with the duties of raising a large family, my mother attended very few baseball games. We were always well fed and went out onto the field in clean uniforms, however. Mom took care of her ball players. At the time we were Little Leaguers, we did not fully appreciate all she did for us to make sure we stepped up to the plate looking our best. My mom's attention and care spoke of her love and dedication.

The same is true of millions of mothers of ballplayers around the world. Moms often keenly anticipate every pitch and cheer every hit by their children. Not just in baseball, but metaphorically, in every part of their kids' lives.

We have a heavenly Mother, too, who looks after all her ballplayers: those who are part of the Lord's team in the spiritual realm. Mary gave birth to our savior, Jesus Christ, in Bethlehem, remaining ever-Virgin. Later, at the foot of the cross, she helped give birth to her spiritual children, the Church, in pain and sorrow.

So, like our earthly mothers who care so deeply for our daily needs, Mary sees to it that we are well nourished on the Bread of Life — the flesh and blood of Jesus. Flesh that came from Mary, the Mother of God, as she has been proclaimed through the ages. Moreover, if we ask her to pray for us, Mary will intercede with her son to grant us his saving grace. For she wants all her spiritual children to show up at the heavenly home plate with a clean uniform — a soul redeemed by Jesus Christ's death and resurrection.

Let us then entrust our brief earthly careers to so good a Mother. Surely, she will attend to our needs in every inning, just as she stepped up to bat for the wedding couple in Cana when they had no wine. Because of her intercession, Jesus turned water into wine and the young couple were spared the embarrassment of striking out with the wedding guests at their reception. May the Blessed Mother, sweet and kind, be with us at every at bat and through every loss and victory.

BALLPLAYER'S PRAYER

O Lord our God, you are the author of all that is good and holy,
We offer you our praise and worship at all times and in all seasons.
Through the creation of ballparks, you show us your power and love;
And through your holy Catholic Church you make us members of your team.
For being devoted to you is our happiness and way to victory.

Accept from our hearts, deepest thanksgiving for your countless blessings;
In baptism you clothed us with the major league uniform of sanctifying grace,
You feed us at the training table of your altar; the Body and Blood of your Son,
Through your Church you forgive our sins, the strike outs and errors we commit,
And through the sacrifice of Jesus your Son, you bring us safely to our eternal home.

We beg your help to never miss a sign from our coach and guide, the Holy Spirit.
Fervently we ask his grace to advance along the base paths of faith, hope, and charity.
By following your commandments may we drive our teammates home.
Teach us to realize that our playing days are short, but we have careers in the next life, eternal,
And that through love and suffering we may be on your roster opening day in the Kingdom.

Amen.

SPIRITUAL MAJOR LEAGUE TRAINING PLAN

We are practicing Catholics, not perfected Catholics. At every minute, every hour of every day we strive to be worthy of our baptismal Major League uniform and to become more like Christ. We have the help of Mary, his holy mother and our mother, and Saint Joseph, his Father on earth and our spiritual father.

As practicing Catholics, we need to keep our final destiny in mind at every stage of our lives: "So teach us to number our days / that we may get a heart of wisdom." (Ps 90:12).

The following spiritual exercises are a constant help in fulfilling our calling as Catholics.

1. Love God above all else. Offer him your time, talent, treasure, and fertility. Be generous.

2. Team is first. God, family, others, and self must be the order of our priorities. Study the Faith and the *Catechism*. You can't give what you don't possess. Many are so cold in their faith because they do not have any deep knowledge of the Faith. It is a universal philosophical and moral principle that one cannot love what one does not know. Even the light and mysterious knowledge of divine faith is necessary for divine charity.

3. Practice acquiring virtue through prayer, fasting, and almsgiving, the triple crown of the saints.

4. Eliminate serious sin from your life. Get a guide as to how to make a good examination of conscience as preparation for the Sacrament of Penance (confession). If you are not strong enough in love for God and your own soul to be serious about the sacraments and repentance, then at least let holy fear move you to do that which is

necessary for your salvation. As the Church insists, if there is not the perfect contrition of love, let there be at least the contrition of fear of judgment and punishment to move to repentance for evil done and avoidance of future evil.

5. Monthly, make a good confession. Work up to this frequency and be motivated by understanding that it is really the Lord Jesus Christ whom you meet in the Sacrament of Penance. He is the One who will judge you at the end of your life, but he is also the savior and mediator with God for all who approach him now. Only in him do we have the hope of final victory, our eternal salvation. As judge and redeemer, it is he who forgives and absolves the sins brought to him in the Sacrament of Penance.

6. Mass on Sunday always — never miss. Acquire a love that will lead you to attending Mass daily.

7. Daily prayer: morning offering, Angelus, Rosary (five decades if you can), fifteen minutes of Scripture reading, evening conscience examination. The depth and effort you put into your prayer life is a measure of how your love for God is growing.

8. Receive our blessed Lord with great love as often as possible.

9. Make a weekly holy hour in church before the tabernacle. Attend an annual three-day silent retreat.

Do all this with the desire of developing and growing intimacy with God. It is he alone who will increase in your soul faith, hope, and love.

Finally, as a Catholic Major Leaguer, consecrate yourself to Saint Joseph!

BASEBALL PARALLELS FOR TEACHING THE FAITH – A THUMBNAIL GUIDE

Here's a summary of the teaching analogies, many presented in the book. I hope it serves as a guide for managers, coaches, or fans who wish to evangelize others through baseballs appeal.

Eye of Faith on the Ball	The Catholic Mysteries in the Ball Park
Baseball	The Eucharistic Host
Bat	Tree in the Garden — the Cross
Home Plate	Heavenly home, our eternal destiny
First, Second, Third Base	Faith, Hope, and Charity, without which home can't be reached
Pitcher's Mound (elevated ground)	Mount Sinai, Old Testament; Sermon on the Mount, New Testament
Three Strikes	Pride, Vanity, Sensuality — three root causes of sin
Four Balls	Four Gospels — Mathew, Mark, Luke, John — leading to faith (first base)
Nine Innings	Length of a Novena — Nine days of prayer before Pentecost
Nine Positions	Nine Choirs of Angels, playing their heavenly positions
Uniform	Baptismal Garment of Grace — God confers to join his team
Cap	Kippah, or yarmulke, with a bill added so we can play in the presence of the Son

Glove	Actual grace equips for our duties in the fielding life's situations
Infield	Sanctuary where the eternal drama unfolds
Base Coaches	Guardian angels to guide the soul on the base paths of life
Outfield — one field — three positions	Trinity — one God — three divine persons
On-deck circle	Personal place of prayer; prepare to advance along the base paths of holiness
Foul Lines	Extend to infinity, evoking the infinite
Foul Poles	Paradoxically indicate a fair ball, raising our eyes to heaven like church spires
Foul Territory	Indicating futility and the powers of darkness
Bench/Bull Pen	Deacons in their role in service to the faithful
Outs	Sins of Omission
Errors	Sins of Commission
Sacrifice	Self–immolation, for the good of others and ourselves
Scoreboard	Examination of Conscience: How well are we playing today's game
Batting Average	The Corporeal Works of Mercy — the Catholic on offense
Earned Run Average	The Spiritual Works of Mercy — defense, fending off evil
Extra-base Hit	Partial Indulgence — advancing on the base path to heaven
Home Run	Plenary Indulgence — touch 'em all clear path to heaven

Stolen Base	Paradoxically a virtue; good thief on the cross steals home
Pinch Hitter	Simon helps Jesus carry his cross
Dugout — bench	Purgatory
Team	Church Militant — those battling for the crown of glory
Injured Reserve	Church Suffering — souls in purgatory
Hall of Famers	Church Triumphant saints in heaven — those who made it to the big show
Triple Crown — Batting	Prayer/Fasting/Almsgiving
Triple Crown — Pitching	Poverty/Chastity/Obedience
Rookie	Beginner who attends Mass at Christmas, Easter, funerals, and weddings
Ace	We can count on Christ for a victory, the devil does not want to face
The Fans	Human Respect, leading to vanity or humility
Pitching/Hitting Coach	Spiritual Director
Manager	The Pastor
Commissioners/Umpires	The Episcopacy
Hall of Fame	Canonized Saints
Spring Training	Lent (meaning spring)
Season longest in sports	Easter — longest liturgical season
Seven-Game Championship Series/World Series	Christmas Octave and Easter Octave

ACKNOWLEDGMENTS

It really is the "ball club" of friends that brought this work to fruition. Thank you to Gina Fickett and my mentor and coach, Author Harold Fickett, for their professional contributions. Thanks as well to Mary Beth Giltner and Scott P. Richert at OSV for their steadfast support.

My gratitude also goes out to my clubhouse buddies Tom Hoopes, Jerry Murrin, Dave and Mari Terhune, Pat Moore, and Scott Brown. I truly appreciate the help or encouragement afforded me along the way over the course of a long season of writing.

Thank you, Fr. Mitch Pacwa, SJ, of EWTN fame for willingness to pour over the manuscript and offer spiritual and theological advice. Fr. Thomas Mary of Jesus, Er.Carm, and Br. John of Jesus and Mary, Er. Carm. offered suggestions and spiritual support. Heartfelt thanks to Tom Thibodeau, a Catholic Major Leaguer, whose constant prodding would not let me be free of the keyboard.

Loving thanks to Mary, my teammate and dedicated wife, who attended all the draft-reading practices and played the extra innings in writing each of the four questions for the meditations. Credit her with a sacrifice fly for moving this runner despite having no real love for baseball. Mother of our five children, she has my vote for the Hall of Fame. In closing, all glory belongs to our blessed Lord with gratitude to Mary, our mother, and Saint Joseph, Jesus' family, and ours!